# EPHESIANS

# WHEN WORLDS COLLIDE

Ed Landry

Published by
Uplifting Christian Books
Nashville, TN

D0888625

Author - Ed Landry
Editorial team- Heidi Henline, Carol Speight, Tom Tucker, David Kennedy and Janet Landry
Book and cover design by the author.
Artwork by David Landry.   http://www.th3anomaly.com/
Additional development team, readers - The Thursday Group (Billy, David and Kathy, Jenny, Lauren, Lorrie, Laura, Rick and Amy, Larry and Patti, John, David, Larry and Doreen, Lisa, Heidi, John, Joe, Rachel, Dan and Lisa, Rick and Connie, Rick and Nancy, Herb and Miraflor).

ISBN-13: 978-0-9990931-1-5

Printed in the United States of America.

# Chapters in Brief

# Introduction
## Ephesians - When Worlds Collide

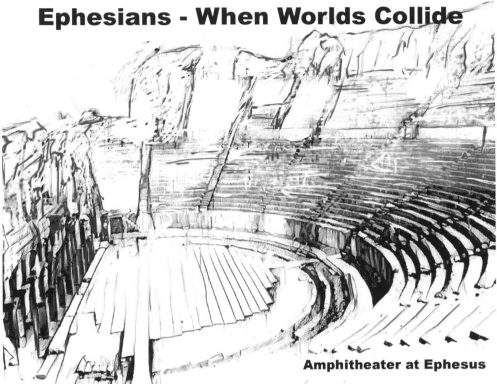

**Amphitheater at Ephesus**

It was one of the greatest cities in the ancient world. Paul had wanted to go there for a long time, and now he was finally on his way. It was his third missionary journey. He had been through so much on his first two adventures. He had been stoned and left for dead, experienced rejection, endured suspicions from the Greeks, the Romans and his own Jewish nation. There was also some conflict within his ministry team. He was imprisoned, suffered many trials and experienced depression. Paul debated the world's greatest philosophers and had confronted pagans and Jewish leaders. But the battles he faced in his first two journeys were only God's boot camp for what was just down the road.

For the next three years, Paul and his company of co-workers would move into the great city of Ephesus. Many worlds were about to collide.

- Jews vs. Gentiles.
- God vs. Satan.
- Idol worshipers vs. the Church.
- Good vs. evil.
- Light vs darkness.
- Ancient, established philosophies vs. God's truth.
- The immoral, occult practices vs. the holy demands of God.
- Conflicts between Greeks, Romans, Jews and believers.

Conflict was in the air. Satan, the prince of this world, had held Ephesus in his grip for centuries, and now the Kingdom of God had arrived and threatened his evil kingdom. It was a war of the worlds.

### Why write another Ephesians commentary?
Numerous commentaries have been written on Ephesians. The purpose of this one is to help pastors and church planters understand the book in a simple way and be able to communicate its timeless message to their churches. For many, the book of Ephesians is complicated and difficult to understand. Personally, I struggled with it for many years. Hopefully this book will help you.

### When was Ephesians written?
The apostle Paul wrote half of the New Testament. Many scholars consider Romans and Ephesians to be his greatest works. Most Biblical scholars agree that the Epistle to the Romans was written around AD 55, and he wrote it while in Corinth, living at the home of Gaius. Ephesians was written later, probably around AD 62 while he was first imprisoned in Rome.

This imprisonment is described in Acts 28:

> "**³⁰ And he stayed two full years in his own rented quarters and was welcoming all who came to him, ³¹ preaching the kingdom of God and teaching concerning the Lord Jesus Christ with all openness, unhindered.**" (Acts 28:30,31)

Paul would later be released and resume his travels and return to many of his earlier church plant locations. He would finally be arrested again and returned to Rome where he would meet his death by beheading, according to tradition, at the hands of Nero, the emperor of Rome. He died around AD 67.

## What do we know about the church at Ephesus?

The church at Ephesus was likely Paul's most effective and strongest church plant. He lived in the city of Ephesus for three years and taught each day at the school of Tyrannus. Paul had a very large and mature church planting team with him at Ephesus. While living there, he discipled young Timothy and eventually turned the work over to him to pastor the church. Paul wrote both the letters of 1 Corinthians and Titus while living in Ephesus.

The New Testament gives us more information about the church in Ephesus than any other church. The impact of this church was felt all over Asia.

> "**⁸ And he entered the synagogue and continued speaking out boldly for three months, reasoning and persuading them about the kingdom of God. ⁹ But when some were becoming hardened and disobedient, speaking evil of the Way before the people, he withdrew from them and took away the disciples, reasoning daily in the school of Tyrannus. ¹⁰ This took place for two years, so that <u>all who lived in Asia heard the word of the Lord, both Jews and Greeks</u>.**" (Acts 19:8-10, emphasis mine)

When John wrote the book of Revelation many years later he recorded the words of Jesus to the seven churches in Asia Minor. The first church Jesus addressed was Ephesus. He commended the church for many godly attributes, but warned them that they had one flaw; they had lost their first love, and they needed to return and do the things they did at first (Revelation 2:1-7). Even after thirty years the church at Ephesus was still a strong and mature church when John recorded Revelation.

The maturity of the believers at Ephesus can be seen throughout the entire letter to the Ephesians. Some of the passages given to them are to this day very difficult for us to understand. The Ephesian believers were a well-taught, well trained, serious body of believers who lived in a hostile, pagan environment. They faced great trials and opposition. Paul gave them special instructions to understand, resist and overcome intense spiritual warfare (Ephesians Six). In Ephesus, the Kingdom of God and the Kingdom of Satan collided, and the war was intense.

## How important was the city of Ephesus?
Ephesus was one of the most important cities in the ancient world. It was built in the 10th century BC and remained under the control and influence of Greece until it came under the rule of the Roman Republic in 129 BC.

The city was well known for its Temple of Artemis (completed around 550 BC), one of the Seven Wonders of the Ancient World. The city also was proud of its large Library of Celsus, and a 25,000-seat outdoor amphitheater which was the site of the riot recorded in the book of Acts.

Ephesus was one of the seven churches of Asia cited in the Book of Revelation. Paul left Timothy in charge of the church of Ephesus and later wrote two letters to him giving him instructions and counsel. Many years later the apostle John became the presiding spiritual leader over the region. The Gospel of John may have been written there.

Ephesus was a significant religious, political, cultural and commercial center in Asia minor (modern day Turkey). The population of the city when Paul walked the streets is estimated at 250,000.

**Library of Celsus**

## The dream team

If you are a pastor or church planter, one of the most important lessons you will learn when you study the church at Ephesus is that planting or shepherding a church is not a one-man show. It is best done by a godly team of dedicated workers.

If you look only at the people Paul worked directly with in his journeys and church plants, the list is over 60. If you add the people

Paul mentions in his letters that he sends greetings to, and if you add the people not directly working with him but influenced by him and then you list all the non-Christians and government leaders he had contact with, then the list is very large.

If church planting had been an Olympic event, this team would have taken the gold medal! Here are some of the prominent names that made up his ministry team: Timothy, Luke, Barnabas, Mark, Apollos, Silas, Titus, Epaphroditus, Priscilla and Aquilla and let's not forget the Apostle John. There are dozens of others he considered his co-workers.

The church is a community of the King. Church planting is a community project. We need each other and nowhere is that more important than in starting a new church. Ephesus was clearly one of the greatest churches in history. It was planted in a very hostile, pagan city that was infested with immorality and cultic worship. This great church grew up in an atmosphere of anger, evil, protest and resistance.

The greatest churches seem to be born in a storm and such was Ephesus. Mix a great God, a dedicated team, a godly leader, a pagan Greek culture, a Roman occupation and a storm of opposition and you have an amazing drama. You have a war. You have a collision of two worlds. So, what happened? What happened was that Jesus built His church and the gates of Hell did not prevail against it.

> **"The people who walk in darkness will see a great light; those who live in a dark land, the light will shine on them."** (Isaiah 9:2)

## A trip to a museum

In America, there is a very famous complex of museums found in the nation's capital. It is called the Smithsonian Institute. It is the world's largest museum, education and research complex, consisting of 19 museums and galleries, the National Zoological Park, and nine research facilities. Suppose you had a chance to visit it, but you only had one hour to see it all. There are 150 million objects on display and there are 20,000 employees and guides to help you but how can you possibly see it all in one hour? It would be totally overwhelming, almost paralyzing. This is why many return again and again to see different parts and continue learning more and more each time. It is a lifetime venture, not a one-hour tour. The same might be said of God. He is not known deeply through a one-time encounter. It takes repeated visits with Him, fellowship with Him, time with Him, to fully get to know Him. Ephesians provides us a chance to get to know Him better.

A subtitle for the first chapter of Ephesians might be – Welcome to the Museum of God.

Now, let's look at that letter, the Epistle to the Ephesians.

**The Temple of Artemis as it looked when Paul was in Ephesus.**

# Ephesians Chapter One

# GOD

## Overview

Maybe you are asking, "Is that the best title you can come up with?" Yes. God is the central theme of the first chapter of Ephesians. He is the the all-consuming fire, the Omni-Omni-Omni God. He is eternal, all knowing, and He is the Supreme guiding power and purpose for the entire universe. He fills the heavens and the earth. He created everything, sustains everything and all of it will ultimately be for His Glory. This chapter basically has two themes; God and prayer. But as you will soon discover, these are not ordinary topics.

# Outline

Chapter One is very deep and broad in its teachings and can be difficult to understand. One way is to teach it in four lessons, just focusing on the general overview of the chapter. Later you may want to expand particular teachings, but a broad overview is helpful at first.

**Section 1 |** Ephesians 1:1-2
Who was Paul?

**Section 2 |** Ephesians 1:3-14 ( Part One)
The most difficult sentence in the Bible!
What Ephesians 1 teaches us about God.

**Section 3 |** Ephesians 1:3-14 (Part Two)
What on Earth has God done?
What Ephesians 1 teaches us about our great salvation.

**Section 4 |** Ephesians 1:15-23
Lord, open our eyes!  Paul's first prayer for the Ephesian believers.

# Commentary

## SECTION 1
## Who was Paul?

**Ephesians 1:1, 2-** Paul's greeting to the believers in Ephesus.

> **"Paul, an apostle of Christ Jesus by the will of God, To the saints who are at Ephesus and who are faithful in Christ Jesus: [2] Grace to you and peace from God our Father and the Lord Jesus Christ. "** (NASB)

### "Hi, this is Paul."

All of Paul's greetings at the beginnings of his letters are usually quite similar. It doesn't mean he uses the same greeting out of habit, but the words he used had very strong meaning to him personally. Paul was a Pharisee, a persecutor of the church, even putting to death those who followed Jesus. He felt this made him a hero (among the Jews), a protector of the law of Moses and the ancient path handed down to Abraham, Isaac and Jacob. He was feared and powerful in the circle of leaders of Judaism in the first century. He was a man of ambition. But God had a different plan!

Forcefully and violently interrupted, Paul's entire life course was changed from being the head persecutor of the church to becoming the greatest church planter of the century. He was a man becoming important in Jewish religious society and growing in authority, but God broke him down in one crushing blow. Paul was ruthless, without mercy and suddenly God flooded his life with truth, understanding and grace. He was a man who formerly followed his own will and now was a man held captive by God's will.

When we first read Paul's greeting it is easy to miss just how important those words were to him. He was thankful he now followed the will of God, not his own destructive path. He was thankful for the grace of God that rescued him from his former life. And he was thankful that his life was at peace with God. For Paul, this was not just a customary greeting, it was the deep expression of his heart.

**\*\*Leader Notes\*\***
In introducing Ephesians take time to go over the life of Paul and his missionary journeys. Here are some suggested points to present in your introduction to Paul:

> **- Paul's religious background: Philippians 3:4-6.**
> **- Paul's persecution of the church and death of Stephen: Acts 7.**
> **- Paul's conversion: Acts 9.**
> **- Paul's life of trial and persecution: 2 Corinthians 11:23-29.**
> **- Trace the three journeys of Paul on a board or handout. Show when he went to Ephesus at the end of his second journey for a visit and then returned for three years at the beginning of his third journey: Acts 18-20.**

# SECTION 2
## The most difficult sentence in the Bible!

**Ephesians 1:3-14 (Part One) -**
What Ephesians One teaches us about God.

Take a few deep breaths before you begin this next section. The first thing to note is that verses 3-14 in the Greek language compose the longest, most complex single sentence in the Bible.

For many, this section is like running into a giant wall.

## Hitting the wall.

Long distance runners like those who run marathons often experience what they call "hitting the wall." It usually occurs late in the race when a person's body begins to run out of needed nutrients. The body's reserves have been used up in the race and the needed energy to strongly finish the race are gone. Mentally, the same thing happens; there is just nothing left. It is frustrating and discouraging. Now try to imagine what a runner would feel like if he hit the wall after only taking a few steps! He would want to quit running.

Reading Ephesians One is like hitting the wall after the first two steps of a race. We immediately encounter a wall the size of a mountain. We confront what may be the most difficult passage found anywhere in Scripture. This explains why Ephesians is a difficult book to read for many. We hit the wall, and we hit it at the beginning and it can be discouraging. We can be tempted to give up.

I recently spoke to the director of a mission agency who has also been a pastor that has spent his entire life teaching the Word of God. He told me his favorite book to teach is Ephesians. I mentioned to him I was writing a simple commentary on Ephesians and that I was working on 1:3-14. Here is what he wrote me later that day:

> *"I love that passage. When you read it out loud, you can actually reproduce the effect by changing a few of the verb tenses to make it into one mind-blowing English sentence. Trouble is, there is too much heavy stuff in that sentence to take it all in...and I end up shutting down mentally...."*

So, if you have had trouble with this section be encouraged — you are not alone.

## What others say about this passage.

> *"It is easy to imagine that Paul is dressed in khakis and a pith helmet, looking like Indiana Jones, taking us on a guided tour through a treasure chamber like those of the Egyptian pharaohs, describing what he sees. He starts out describing the most immediate and evident facts - then something else comes into view and he shines his lantern on it. Then comes some new glorious object or artifact, and glory flashes upon glory until he has compiled a dazzlingly complex sentence describing the vast and nearly indescribable riches of the chamber."* Ray Stedman

> *"I do not hesitate to assert that we have in this passage the key to understanding the chief practical purpose of the letter to the Ephesians, even more- the entire message of the Bible."* Martin Lloyd Jones

> *"Ephesians 1:3-14 is like one of those rushing streams that looks easy to wade in but sweeps us off our feet by its sheer flowing power."* Luther Seminary staff commentary

Before we look into this amazing passage it is helpful to be reminded that the Bible is different from all other books in the world. It is the only book that is inspired by the living God. I think it is helpful to briefly remind ourselves what inspiration means before we read Ephesians 1:3-14.

## The wind of God - Understanding inspiration.

> *"All Scripture is inspired by God and is useful to teach us what is true and to make us realize what is wrong in our*

**lives. It corrects us when we are wrong and teaches us to do what is right. [17]so that the man of God may be adequate, equipped for every good work."** (2 Timothy 3:16, 17)

**"[20] Above all, you must realize that no prophecy in Scripture ever came from the prophet's own understanding, [21] or from human initiative. No, those prophets were moved by the Holy Spirit, and they spoke from God."** (2 Peter 1:20, 21)

Two important words in the Greek language help us to understand what inspiration means. The first word *(theopneustos)* translated "inspired" in 2 Timothy 3:16 means "divinely breathed in." It describes the work of inspiration as the breath of God entering God's appointed servant directing and protecting the very words spoken by the man of God.

The second word *(pherō)* found in 2 Peter 1:21 is the word translated "moved." It is a word rich in meaning and helps us understand more about the process of inspiration. The word describes being carried along by a mighty storm, a great gust of wind filling the sails of a ship and moving it.

A wonderful picture of that word is found in the following passage about the shipwreck of the Apostle Paul found in Acts 27. The word *(pherō)* is used twice and gives us a powerful illustration of the process of inspiration.

### Acts 27:13-17 (NLT)

**"[13] When a light wind began blowing from the south, the sailors thought they could make it. So they pulled up anchor and sailed close to the shore of Crete. [14] But the weather changed abruptly, and a wind of typhoon strength (called a "northeaster") burst across the island and blew us out to sea. [15] The sailors couldn't turn the ship into the wind, so they gave up and let it run before the gale."** *(pherō).*

1:3-14

"¹⁶ We sailed along the sheltered side of a small island named Cauda, where with great difficulty we hoisted aboard the lifeboat being towed behind us. ¹⁷ Then the sailors bound ropes around the hull of the ship to strengthen it. They were afraid of being driven across to the sandbars of Syrtis off the African coast, so they lowered the sea anchor to slow the ship and were driven before the wind." *(pherō)*.

## The wind was irresistible and they let it drive the ship where it would take them.

So why is it important to review this before we enter this next section of Ephesians Chapter One? Ephesians 1:3-14 is about God. It tells us about His nature, His attributes, His works and His heart. God is telling us about Himself, and we can trust it is true because the very breath of God filled the mind of the Apostle Paul and gave us words that no man could know unless God Himself revealed it to him.

> **"For as the heavens are higher than the earth,**
> **So are My ways higher than your ways**
> **And My thoughts than your thoughts."** (Isaiah 55:9)

This is why the passage is so hard to understand. It is also why the passage is so important and worth the time to study it. The same God who inspired it loves to help us understand it as we are faithful to study His word (2 Tim 2:15).

My friend's experience with this passage is actually common. Most of us shut down mentally trying to understand it. So before we take a look at Ephesians 1:3-14, **I want you to keep the following three things in mind as you read it:**

1. The passage can be actually divided into three sections based on the Trinity. Verses 3-6 focuss on God the Father, verses 7-12 on God the Son, and verses 13 and 14 on the Holy Spirit.

**2.** At least 35 major doctrines are introduced or used in this one sentence.

**3.** For God to inspire Paul to give the church in Ephesus such depth of teaching is an indication of the maturity of the Ephesian believers. In contrast to the strong church of Ephesus is the church in Corinth that Paul planted just before the Ephesian Church. Corinth was a carnal church, living in sin, arrogant, disobedient to God and lacking faith to follow God and even believe in the resurrection. Both Ephesus and Corinth were pagan cities with pagan temples, and both were under Roman control. In spite of many similarities, one was weak and carnal, and the other was strong and mature even though both had been established by the same group of godly men and women. So when you read Ephesians you are not only getting the meaty teachings; you are getting the crown jewels of God.

Now, just read it without stopping, the same way it was inspired and written down. Let the sheer length, width and depth flood over you.

### Ephesians 1:3-14 – Buckle your seatbelts!!

"³ Blessed be the God and Father of our Lord Jesus Christ, who has blessed us with every spiritual blessing in the heavenly places in Christ, ⁴ just as He chose us in Him before the foundation of the world, that we would be holy and blameless before Him. In love ⁵He predestined us to adoption as sons through Jesus Christ to Himself, according to the kind intention of His will, ⁶ to the praise of the glory of His grace, which He freely bestowed on us in the Beloved. ⁷ In Him we have redemption through His blood, the forgiveness of our trespasses, according to the riches of His grace ⁸ which He lavished on us. In all wisdom and insight ⁹ He made known to us the mystery of His will, according to

His kind intention which He purposed in Him [10] with a view to an administration suitable to the fullness of the times, that is, the summing up of all things in Christ, things in the heavens and things on the earth. In Him [11] also we have obtained an inheritance, having been predestined according to His purpose who works all things after the counsel of His will, [12] to the end that we who were the first to hope in Christ would be to the praise of His glory. [13] In Him, you also, after listening to the message of truth, the gospel of your salvation—having also believed, you were sealed in Him with the Holy Spirit of promise, [14] who is given as a pledge of our inheritance, with a view to the redemption of God's own possession, to the praise of His glory."

Yes, that was one sentence, one continuous thought in the Greek!

**In case you were wondering here is a list of major doctrines used in this one sentence:**

- God the Father
- God the Son
- The person and work of God the Holy Spirit
- Different functions within the Trinity
- Our position and benefits of being in Christ
- Election, chosen from the foundation of the earth
- The foreknowledge of God
- Predestination of God
- Creation by God
- Holiness
- Righteousness, blameless before God
- The Love of God
- Adoption as sons of God
- The will of God
- The kindness of God
- The glory of God
- The grace of God
- The wisdom of God
- The omniscience of God

1:3-14

- Redemption
- Efficacy of the blood of Christ
- Forgiveness of sins
- Mystery of God's will
- The administration of God over the affairs of man (some call dispensations)
- The supremacy of Christ
- Heaven and earth
- Our eternal inheritance in Christ
- God's omnipotence and omnipresence
- The purpose of man
- The Gospel
- Salvation
- Faith, belief
- The sealing of the Holy Spirit
- Believers, the possession of God
- Praise and worship of God

Aren't you happy you didn't get a school assignment to write one sentence that contained all of those 35 doctrines?

If verses one and two could be seen as Paul introducing himself, "Hi, this is Paul," then verses 3-14 can be seen as God saying, **"Hi, this is God!"**

Hundreds of commentaries have been written on each of these doctrines. Wars have been fought, churches have split, denominations have begun, and yet we are probably no closer to understanding the depths of these verses than in the first century.

> **"For now we see only a reflection as in a mirror; then we shall see face to face. Now I know in part; then I shall know fully, even as I am fully known."** (1 Cor. 13:12)

> **"For my thoughts are not your thoughts,**

1:3-14

**neither are your ways my ways, declares the Lord."**
(Isaiah 55:8)

I know what you are now waiting for. You want answers to the following questions:

*- Aren't you going to explain predestination and free will. How can they possibly go together?*

*- What about the foreknowledge of God? Some people like Open Theists believe man's free will determines the future and God has a limited amount of knowledge. Arminians and Calvinists present totally opposite views on just about every-thing related to God's knowledge, His sovereignty and man's free will. So who is right?*

During the early 18th century two well-known preachers had a public dispute over these questions and remained divided their entire lives. George Whitefield and John Wesley both were influential preachers, yet they could not bridge the gap in their theological differences. Whitefield was a Calvinist and Wesley an Arminian. A story is told of a newspaper reporter interviewing Whitefield when he asked him if he thought he would see John Wesley in Heaven. Whitefield answered, "No, I won't." The reporter sensed he had a sensational story to report until he heard Whitefield's next statement. "John Wesley will be so close to the throne of Jesus that I will not see him through the crowd!"

Maybe we all need a good dose of humility and grace when we deal with others regarding subjects like these. Have you ever thought that God just might be greater than all of man's attempts to explain Him? Have you ever considered that God can put together things we can't, like His sovereignty and man's free will? In the book of Job, God spent four chapters at the end of the book showing Job how much Job didn't understand. Job's response was,

> **"Surely I spoke of things I did not understand, things too wonderful for me to know."** (Job 42:3)

**Remember, this book is intended to be an overview.**
My purpose is not to write one more book about all these doctrines. There are thousands already. I want you to see that God has in essence given us an abbreviated autobiography about His nature and purpose and has displayed the crown jewels of salvation and the church in this incredible passage. I hope it will drive you to dig deeper and marvel more and more about our great God. Chapter One verses 3-14 is like a museum of God, and we need to go back time and again to visit the exhibits, and each time we will learn more.

**\*\*Leader Notes\*\***
I mentioned earlier that you might consider handling all of Chapter One in four lessons. The first was Paul's introduction.

**Now here are suggested lesson outline topics for sections 2 and 3 which deal with Ephesians 1:3-14.**

---

# SECTION 2
## What Ephesians One teaches us about God – a brief survey.
- Share what inspiration of Scripture means.
- The Trinity and nature of God and creation.
- The attributes of God, omniscience, omnipotence and omnipresence.
- The sovereignty of God over the affairs of man.
- Understanding the hard topics of election, predestination and foreknowledge.

- The role of the Holy Spirit in salvation and the church.

## SECTION 3
## What on earth has God done? – Our great salvation – a brief survey.

- What is the Gospel?
- What is sin?
- What is saving faith?
- What is salvation?
- What does it mean to be adopted by God?
- What is the role of the Holy Spirit in convicting, regenerating and sealing the believer in the body of Christ?
- What does it mean to be "in Christ?"
- What does redemption mean?

Once again, I suggest you give a large overview of what it means to be a sinner saved by grace and lift up the God of our salvation. It may not be necessary to do exhaustive studies of each of these topics at first, but present them as a sweeping overview of our great sovereign God who alone is worthy of our worship. This is about God, so focus on the greatness of God and his works.

Remember, theologians have written volumes on each of these topics. Many disputes in the church have been fought over these great truths. At the same time, millions of believers have been stirred and encouraged as they have meditated on the greatness of God and marveled at His works and grace in our lives.

If we did nothing but pray this passage back to God each day of our lives we would praise him more each day and still never come to a full understanding of the greatness and grace of our Creator, Savior and Sustainer of our lives.

One thing that this passage did for Paul was cause him to pray for his people. That is the topic of the final section of this chapter.

# Section 4
## Lord, open our eyes!

### Ephesians 1:15-23 – Paul's first prayer for the Ephesian believers.

After Paul presents the immense and almost overwhelming description of God and His amazing salvation, he then ends the chapter by praying for the Ephesian believers. He wants them to know God more, and he prays that their eyes would be opened wider than ever before to understand the great revelation he has just given them. His prayer reveals how much he loved the church at Ephesus. He wanted them to marvel at the greatness of God and more than anything to truly grasp the wondrous things our Lord had done for them.

The prayer also serves as a great model of how a pastor or teacher should pray for their people.

Let's read the prayer and then look at it in more detail.

### Paul's prayer.

"[15] For this reason I too, having heard of the faith in the Lord Jesus which exists among you and your love for all the saints, [16] do not cease giving thanks for you, while making mention of you in my prayers; [17] that the God of our Lord Jesus Christ, the Father of glory, may give to you a spirit of wisdom and of revelation in the knowledge of Him. [18] I pray that the eyes of your heart may be enlightened, so that you will know what is the hope of His calling, what are the riches of the glory of His inheritance in the saints, [19] and what is the surpassing greatness of His power toward us who believe. These are in accordance with the working of the strength of His might [20] which He brought about in Christ,

when He raised Him from the dead and seated Him at His right hand in the heavenly places, [21] far above all rule and authority and power and dominion, and every name that is named, not only in this age but also in the one to come. [22] And He put all things in subjection under His feet, and gave Him as head over all things to the church, [23] which is His body, the fullness of Him who fills all in all."
(Ephesians 1:15-23)

The greatness of God and the wonder of salvation as revealed in verses 3-14 are immediately followed by Paul's desire to pray for the church in Ephesus. Paul had to pray for those who read it. He wanted God to help them understand all that had been written. He prayed that God Himself would guide them and teach them what had been revealed. This first of two prayers in the book of Ephesians is a prayer for enlightenment, understanding and wisdom. The second prayer found in Chapter Three will be a prayer for empowerment, the spiritual strength to live the Christian life in a pagan and hostile world. Both prayers are great examples of how Christian leaders can pray for their people.

**Now, Let's examine the prayer in Chapter One.**

## Ephesians 1:15,16

"[15]For this reason I too, having heard of the faith in the Lord Jesus which exists among you and your love for all the saints, [16]do not cease giving thanks for you, while making mention of you in my prayers;"

Paul rejoices to hear that the faith of the Ephesian believers has remained strong in light of the intense local persecution by the pagan idol worshippers of the Temple of Artemis. Sometimes it is easy to see problems and defeats. But here Paul is encouraged by the good reports he had received.

The love the body has shown each other is also a great testimony to the strength of the church. For Paul, it was a joy to see how his three years of investment in the lives of the Ephesian believers had been worth it. For all pastors and teachers, don't grow weary in your calling even when opposition becomes strong. Pastor, do you focus on problems or do you take the time to thank God often for the ones God has put under your leadership? Paul never stopped giving thanks for the church in Ephesus. He even found things to praise God for with the troubled church in Corinth. It has been said that a pessimist sees a glass half empty while an optimist sees it half full. What do you see when you look at your church?

## Ephesians 1:17

> **"that the God of our Lord Jesus Christ, the Father of glory, may give to you a spirit of wisdom and of revelation in the knowledge of Him."**

A passage found in **James 1:5** instructs us:

> **"But if any of you lacks wisdom, let him ask of God, who gives to all generously and without reproach, and it will be given to him."**

It is a prayer we all need to pray. In verse 17 Paul asks for wisdom and understanding for his church. When we encounter a difficult passage like Ephesians 1:3-14, we need direct help from the Author Himself. One of the roles of the Holy Spirit is to guide and teach us, so Paul calls on the Heavenly Teacher to help his people understand the inspired word God has just given them. After all who knows more about the things of God than the Spirit of God Himself.

> **For to us God revealed them through the Spirit; for the Spirit searches all things, even the depths of God.**
> (1 Cor. 2:10)

Paul continues,

**Ephesians 1:18**

> **"I pray that the eyes of your heart may be enlightened, so that you will know what is the hope of His calling, what are the riches of the glory of His inheritance in the saints,"**

Have you ever had a wonderful experience in your life and your first thought was that you wished someone you knew could have been there to experience it as well? Paul had been caught up in the breath of God like a mighty wind that fills the sails of a great ship. In that burst of inspiration he was made to understand many deep things of God. His prayer in verse 18 indicates he wished his beloved Ephesian church could have the same experience of understanding. Listen to his prayer again:

> **"I pray that the eyes of your heart may be enlightened, so that <u>you will know</u> what is the hope of His calling, what are the riches of the glory of His inheritance in the saints,"** (emphasis mine)

He is saying, *"Lord open their eyes wide and fill their understanding with Your Spirit and increase their wonder of Your sovereign calling in their lives and the glorious inheritance we have as Your children."* Good parents like to provide their children with an inheritance when they die. It is an act of love. God's riches are infinite, far beyond measure or human understanding. The death of Jesus, the Son of God, provided to all of us as believers who have been adopted into the family of God, the rights as full children of God. We are inheritors of the riches of God. Paul's prayer is for us to better understand what all that means.

**Ephesians 1:19-23**

> **"[19] and what is the surpassing greatness of His power toward us who believe. These are in accordance with the**

working of the strength of His might [20] which He brought about in Christ, when He raised Him from the dead and seated Him at His right hand in the heavenly places, [21] far above all rule and authority and power and dominion, and every name that is named, not only in this age but also in the one to come. [22] And He put all things in subjection under His feet, and gave Him as head over all things to the church, [23] which is His body, the fullness of Him who fills all in all."

This last section of Paul's prayer lifts the believers out of the filth and hopelessness around them and into the presence of the resurrected King Jesus. He is seated at the right hand of majesty in heaven. He is above all earthly rulers and rulers in the darkness of the fallen spiritual world. His authority is supreme and his rule is eternal. All other authorities on earth are under our King. He is the only leader worthy to follow and He is the head of the church.

We have nothing to fear, our King is with us and will never forsake us. And the same God that raised Jesus from the dead has raised us from the dead and seated us with Christ. We were dead in our sins, without hope, deceived by the enemy, slaves of sin and under the wrath of God . . . but God, rich in mercy saved us and lifted us out of our helpless condition, gave us life eternal and changed everything for us forever. Praise God!

People want to have leadership they can trust. It is difficult to play for a sports team when the coach is not respected or his decisions seem biased or foolish. It is frustrating to work for a company when the boss is mean, dishonest, or unsympathetic to the workers. It is hard to have confidence in a government election when candidates are corrupt or election fraud is happening. We want honesty, fairness and godly leadership.

The Roman government was a strong, dictatorial ruling force and the local leadership of the city was pagan and immoral. So Paul reminds the church of Ephesus just who they are following. The church has a different leader who is the Prince of princes, the King of kings and the Lord of all lords. The church can live victoriously in the dark world because we have the Light of the world in charge.

**\*\*Leader Notes\*\***
As mentioned, 35 major doctrines were listed that are found in verses 3-14. In Paul's prayer he adds a few more. Each of these topics can be expanded and explained to your people.

- Prayer.
- Wisdom from God.
- The revelation of God, wisdom and knowledge comes from Him.
- Hope comes from God.
- Our eternal inheritance as children of God, the riches of God.
- The power of God available to all who believe.
- The resurrection of Christ.
- Our position in Christ, seated with Him at the right hand of God the Father.
- The supremacy of Christ.
- The deity, rule and eternity of Christ.
- The Church and headship of Christ.

Here is how one preacher reminded his people about the King we serve:

## My King by S.M. Lockridge.

"I'm here to tell you,
The heavens cannot contain Him,
let alone a man explain Him.
You can't get Him out of your mind.
You can't get Him off of your hands.
You can't outlive Him and you can't live without Him.
The Pharisees couldn't stand Him,

but they found they couldn't stop him.
Pilate couldn't fault Him.
Herod couldn't kill Him.
Death couldn't conquer Him
and the grave couldn't hold Him!
That's my King!   Yeah
He has always been and always will be;
He had no predecessor and
will have no successor;
You can't impeach Him and
he isn't going to resign!
His name is above every name;
That at the name of Jesus
Every knee shall bow
Every tongue shall confess
That Jesus Christ is Lord!
His is the kingdom,
and the power,
and the glory...
forever, and ever and ever and ever.
Hallelujah! . . . and Amen!"

# Summary of Chapter One

Once again, it is not my purpose in producing this book to write another commentary about all the incredible doctrines contained in Ephesians. It is to give you an overview of Ephesians and, hopefully, an appetite to study the book further. It is also to provide some suggestions of how to teach the book to others. It is generally helpful to give others a basic overview of the entire work before you begin looking at details. This is the basic overview. It is up to you to develop the details.

I compared chapter One to being in a great museum where all the exhibits are about God and His church. I truly hope you will return again and again to spend time in that museum. And don't forget, the museum of God is open 24 hours a day and admission is free!

# Ephesians Chapter Two

MAN
from darkness to light

## Overview

Chapter One was primarily about God. Chapter Two begins with man and the darkness and desperation of the human heart before Christ changes it. The big message of Chapter Two is grace. After man is introduced in a hopeless and helpless condition, God steps in and changes everything by His grace. And He doesn't stop there. God makes a new man, a church, a special community of believers made up of both Jew and Gentile by breaking down all former barriers and prejudices that had kept them apart. This is what happens when the kingdoms of this world meet the kingdom of the living God.

# Outline

**Section 1** | Ephesians 2:1-3
Man, a journey to the dark side.

**Section 2** | Ephesians 2:4-10
Two words that changed everything. Amazing grace, how sweet the sound.

**Section 3** | Ephesians 2:11-22
A wall only God could break down.

# Commentary

---

## SECTION 1
## Man, a journey to the dark side.

**Ephesians 2:1-3**

> "And you were dead in your trespasses and sins, ² in which you formerly walked according to the course of this world, according to the prince of the power of the air, of the spirit that is now working in the sons of disobedience. ³ Among them we too all formerly lived in the lusts of our flesh, indulging the desires of the flesh and of the mind, and were by nature children of wrath, even as the rest."

These first three verses give us a very dark picture of man. In Chapter Two Paul reminds the Ephesian believers about the beauty of God's grace. But to do that effectively, he had to first remind them what they were like before they were saved. He paints a vivid picture of their hearts and the heart of every man. And it is not a pretty portrait. Here are four words that describe what these verses teach us about unsaved man. He is Dead, Deceived, Depraved and Doomed. Let's take a closer look.

### Dead!

> "And you were dead in your trespasses and sins,"
> (Ephesians 2:1)

Spiritually dead towards God. Sin has completely separated us from life, from God. What can a dead person do to help himself? We can't give ourselves life; only God can do that. I am so thankful that our Savior is the "resurrection and the life." Only He can produce life where there is only death and decay. Jesus is the one that called Lazarus from the tomb, and that is what He has done with our dead spirit. We have been made alive in Christ. Paul tells the Ephesians you "were" dead. It is past tense. We who believe are now no longer dead, but raised by Him to eternal life.

> **"Truly, truly, I say to you, he who hears My word, and believes Him who sent Me, has eternal life, and does not come into judgment, but has passed out of death into life."** (John 5:24)

There are some today that teach man is really not all that bad. They say he has the spark of the divine inside and all we have do is fan it into flame. But that is not the picture Ephesians gives us. You can fan a corpse all day long but you won't find a spark of life. Only the One who said He is the resurrection and the life can help someone who is dead.

## Deceived!

> **"in which you formerly walked according to the course of this world, according to the prince of the power of the air, of the spirit that is now working in the sons of disobedience."** (Ephesians 2:2)

Not only were we dead in our sins, but we were slaves of Satan, the prince and power of the air. The Bible teaches that "the **whole world** lies in *the power of* the **evil** one" (1 John 5:19, emphasis mine). He is the great deceiver, a liar from the beginning, and we all followed his lead along with the rest of the world. He deceives, and then he accuses us before God. He is also described as a vicious roaring lion devouring everyone he can. This is the one we followed before we trusted Christ.

2:1-3

One of his greatest deceptions is religion. He specializes in getting people to follow religion instead of having a true relationship with Christ. The Pharisees were very religious and felt they were doing everything right, but Jesus rebuked them time and again for their hypocrisy. Some feel that attending a particular church or doing a certain good deed makes them a Christian but Jesus warns those that they too have been deceived.

> [21]"Not everyone who says to Me, 'Lord, Lord,' will enter the kingdom of heaven, but he who does the will of My Father who is in heaven will enter. [22]Many will say to Me on that day, 'Lord, Lord, did we not prophesy in Your name, and in Your name cast out demons, and in Your name perform many miracles?' [23] And then I will declare to them, 'I never knew you; depart from Me, you who practice lawlessness.'"
> (Matthew 7:21-23)

So, we have seen we are dead and deceived, without life and light. That brings us to the third thing we learn about our life before Christ:

## Depraved!

> ". . . among them we too all formerly lived in the lusts of our flesh, indulging the desires of the flesh and of the mind."
> (Ephesians 2:3)

Today, there are popular teachers and pastors who teach that even though we experience the results of the Fall, we are basically good at heart. Is man basically good and our job is to bring out that goodness? Or is man basically broken and without God's intervention we are without hope? Ephesians Two and other passages in God's Word clearly support the second view. Many Scriptures reveal that we are all born sinners and that sin has infected every part of us.

2:1-3

For a moment let's consider the topic of human depravity, or to put it in other words, just how bad or broken are we? Not all Christians agree on this. A recent survey among Christians in America by the top Christian research agency found that 77 percent of those calling themselves Christians believe man is basically good, not bad. But our theology is not determined by popular belief or polls. It is determined by the Word of God. So, what do we see in the Bible about man?

## A few of the many Scriptures which describe the nature of man:

> "The LORD saw that the wickedness of man was great in the earth, and that every intention of the thoughts of his heart was only evil continually." (Genesis 6:5)

> "Can the Ethiopian change his skin or the leopard its spots? Neither can you do good who are accustomed to doing evil." (Jeremiah 13:23)

> "None is righteous, no, not one; no one understands; no one seeks for God." (Romans 3:10-11)

> "For the mind that is set on the flesh is hostile to God, for it does not submit to God's law; indeed, it cannot. Those who are in the flesh cannot please God. You, however, are not in the flesh but in the Spirit, if in fact the Spirit of God dwells in you. Anyone who does not have the Spirit of Christ does not belong to him." (Romans 8:7-9)

> "The natural person does not accept the things of the Spirit of God, for they are folly to him, and he is not able to understand them because they are spiritually discerned." (1 Corinthians 2:14)

In Ephesians Chapter Four we will later see that apart from the work of Christ in a person's life, all mankind are:

"...darkened in their understanding, alienated from the life of God because of the ignorance that is in them, due to their hardness of heart." (Eph. 4:18)

Or, as Jesus said,

"Apart from me you can do nothing." (John 15:5)

Total depravity does not mean that human beings are as bad as they possibly could be. Total depravity means that no part of our being remains untouched and unaffected by the corruption of sin. Sin has enslaved the total person.

The absolute depravity of fallen man is usually associated with Calvinism, but it was also the view of James Arminius the founder of what is called Arminianism. Here are his views on the condition of fallen man:

"In this state, the Free Will of man towards the True Good is not only wounded, maimed, infirm, bent, and weakened [attenuatem]; but it is also imprisoned [captivatum], destroyed and lost. And its powers are not only debilitated and useless unless they be assisted by grace, but it has no powers whatever except such as are excited by Divine grace..."

In writing about the views of John Wesley, an Arminian, one Wesleyan theologian has said,

"Wesley maintains that natural man is totally corrupt." He is "sinful through and through, has no knowledge of God and no power to turn to him of his own free will."

Calvinists and Arminians represent most of the Christian world and do have differing views of many things, but in this one thing they do agree. Man is not basically good but is desperately broken and apart from God's intervention he will remain in that helpless

2:1-3

state and deserves the wrath of God. Without Christ we are dead, deceived and depraved. That brings us to the fourth word we are looking at in Ephesians 2:1-3:

## Doomed!

> "... and were by nature children of wrath, even as the rest."
> (Ephesians 2:3)

Have you noticed the logical flow of these three verses in Chapter Two? We are dead to God, and therefore we fall into deception from our enemy, Satan. This leads to a life of sin and depravity and because of this we come under the judgment of God, his wrath. We are doomed.

Sometimes unbelievers mock the Bible and God by saying God must be unloving to send people to Hell. How can God permit any person to go to Hell? But when we understand the holiness of God and the absolute rebellion of man, maybe the better question should be, "How can God permit any person to go to heaven?" The next passage in Ephesians 2 will answer that question, it is about grace. But before we get to that, let's take a brief look at the topic of the wrath of God we see in Ephesians 2:3.

## The wrath of God.

The wrath of God is just, it is righteous.

> "But because of your hard and impenitent heart you are storing up wrath for yourself on the day of wrath when God's righteous judgment will be revealed." (Romans 2:5)

The difference between the wrath of man and the wrath of God is that with God it is Holy, and it is in all cases justified. Both Old and New Testaments describe the wrath of God. It is God's reaction to sin and disobedience (Psalm 78:56-66, Deuteronomy 1:26-46, Joshua 7:1, Psalm 2:1-6 and Zephaniah 1:14-15 are examples in the Old testament). The New Testament continues that same theme.

> **"Whoever believes in the Son has eternal life, but whoever rejects the Son will not see life, for God's wrath remains on Him."** (John 3:36)

For the unbeliever, it is a terrifying thing.

> **". . . when the Lord Jesus shall be revealed from heaven with his mighty angels, [8] In flaming fire taking vengeance on them that know not God, and that obey not the gospel of our Lord Jesus Christ: [9] Who shall be punished with everlasting destruction from the presence of the Lord, and from the glory of his power."** (2 Thessalonians 1:7-9)

But for the believer we have been delivered from His wrath because Jesus bore the wrath of God in our place on the cross.

> **"Since we have now been justified by His blood, how much more shall we be saved from God's wrath through Him!"** (Romans 5:9)

To summarize Ephesians 2:1-3 Paul is saying, "Fellow believers in Christ, I want to share with you the wonderful grace of God. But before we talk about grace, we need to be reminded of what we were before God graciously touched our lives and changed us into his children. We didn't deserve God's grace and mercy because we were enemies of the living God. We were born dead, cut off from God. We were led deeply into sin, deceived by Satan and became participators in the darkest and vilest of sin, driven by our fallen nature and were completely unable to rescue ourselves from our slavery to sin. We were on the highway to Hell.

But then something happened, something changed everything,

something undeserved, something unexpected.  What was it?
Verse four will now answer that question, and it begins with just
two words, two words that change everything.

---

# SECTION 2
## "But God" . . . two words that changed everything.

### Ephesians 2:4-10

When we get to verse four everything changes. It begins with two
small words, "But God . . ." The first three verses were all doom and
gloom "But God . . ." Man, in his natural state, is desperately lost with
no hope of freeing himself from his lost condition. But with God in the
story everything changes.

> You were dead, helpless, lost . . . . "But God. . ."
> You lived in deception, a child of the Devil . . . "But God. . . "
> You were a powerless slave of sin . . . "But God . . . "
> You were under the wrath of God, doomed forever . . . "But
> God."

Now because of those two words we get to add one more "D" word,
**"Delivered!"** Thank you, God.

God steps in and the fog of evil, sin and darkness lifts, and hope and
grace flood in. These two words sum up the entire Bible. Man was
created, man sinned and cut himself off from his Creator.

### . . . But God . . .

One of the more graphic pictures of our helpless condition and the
loving heart of God is found in Ezekiel 16, and I highly recommend
you go back and read it. God tells Israel that He rescued them from
a helpless death. He describes them like an unwanted newborn
child tossed out into a field and left to die, covered in blood and

lying naked in the dirt. God sees him squirming in his own blood and rescues him and nurtures him back to life. He covers his shame with fine clothing and adopts him into his royal family and feeds him with the finest of foods. Israel was dying as a filthy, helpless, abandoned baby . . . But God. . . It is our story as well isn't it?

Now let's look at the entire passage about grace.

### Delivered! - Ephesians 2:4-10

Amazing Grace, how sweet the sound.

> "[4] But God, being rich in mercy, because of His great love with which He loved us, [5] even when we were dead in our transgressions, made us alive together with Christ (by grace you have been saved), [6] and raised us up with Him, and seated us with Him in the heavenly places in Christ Jesus, [7] so that in the ages to come He might show the surpassing riches of His grace in kindness toward us in Christ Jesus. [8] For by grace you have been saved through faith; and that not of yourselves, it is the gift of God; [9] not as a result of works, so that no one may boast. [10] For we are His workmanship, created in Christ Jesus for good works, which God prepared beforehand so that we would walk in them."

When we are at our weakest, God's power rushes to our aid.

> "And He has said to me, "My grace is sufficient for you, for power is perfected in weakness." Most gladly, therefore, I will rather boast about my weaknesses, so that the power of Christ may dwell in me." (2 Corinthians 12:9)

So this passage makes perfect sense when we understand the loving and merciful heart of God. Man is dead, deceived, depraved and doomed. What is God's response? Deliverance by grace. Look at it again.

> "⁴ But God, being rich in mercy, because of His great love with which He loved us, ⁵ even when we were dead in our transgressions, made us alive together with Christ (by grace you have been saved), ⁶ and raised us up with Him, and seated us with Him in the heavenly places in Christ Jesus." (Ephesians 2:4-6)

Man is dead in his sins. God gives him life, resurrection life.

Man is deceived and depraved, helpless in his sin and unable to free himself from the pit of despair he is in. God lifts him up after giving him resurrection life and brings him into the very presence of the living God. He is taken from the trash heap of this world and placed in the holy and pure heavenly presence of God himself. Man's lifeless spirit has been rescuscitated by the breath of God.

Man is doomed, under wrath, because of his sin and God saves him. Jesus bore the wrath of the Father on the cross in our place and now we are no longer under wrath. When Jesus said "It is finished," He meant exactly that. Instead of wrath we now have grace.

**Several phrases and words from this passage need further explanation so below are three helpful insights:**

## INSIGHT 1
**What does it mean to be seated with Christ in heavenly places?**

This is one of those phrases that Christians see in different ways.

1 Some see that when Christ died and finished the work of salvation the Scripture says He was seated at the right hand of the Father. We are told we are in Christ when we become believers, therefore, we are with Him as He is seated in the Heavenlies.

It is a past tense statement. We are seated, not **will be** seated. When He took His place, we, being in Christ, did also. So, it can be describing a positional relationship. Our place is secure and with Him just as much as the day when we will finally be there in person.

2 Some see it as God is infinite, eternal, all-knowing and is everywhere - past, present and future. He is not subject to time like we are. The past and future are the same to Him. He said His name is "I Am." Not I was, and I will be, but "I Am." He knew us before time and called us to Himself before creation. He is already present 1,000 years from now, and we are seated with Him in the Heavenlies. To God it is not something that will happen in the future. To God it is all the present even if it still future for us.

I know some of that is hard to understand but just reading the words that we are already seated with Him is wonderful news. The answer is found in God, and we know His thoughts and ways are far above us. The main thing on difficult passages like this is to trust God and rejoice in Him, and one day it will be clearer than when we struggled with these things on earth.

## INSIGHT 2
**What is the difference between grace and mercy?**

This passage uses both words, grace and mercy. They are both extensions or results from the love of God.

> **Mercy is not getting what we deserve.**
> **Grace is getting what we don't deserve.**

### Mercy
– A condemned criminal deserves a long sentence in prison. But a judge decides to show mercy on him by reducing his

2:8-10

sentence. His crime deserves a strong punishment, he deserves it, but mercy did not give him what he deserved.

**Grace**

- A young street kid grows up without parents to guide him. He steals some food from a local vendor. He is caught by the owner. The owner shows mercy by not turning him over to the police, (He didn't get what he deserved, he was spared imprisonment). But the owner goes further. He provides a wonderful meal for the child and gives him money for some future meals (that would be a loving act) but he then has great compassion on the child and arranges to adopt the child into his family and give him the family name and makes him an heir of all the owner has. That is getting what he did not deserve, that is grace and that is what God has done for us.

We have been spared from the wrath of God, shown mercy, and we have been blessed beyond anything we could ever deserve or even dream of. We have become recipients of God's grace.

---

## INSIGHT 3
**Ephesians 2:8-10 - Faith and works.**

> "[8] **For by grace you have been saved through faith; and that not of yourselves, it is the gift of God;** [9] **not as a result of works, so that no one may boast.** [10] **For we are His workmanship, created in Christ Jesus for good works, which God prepared beforehand so that we would walk in them.**"

Over the centuries, Christians have struggled with understanding the relationship between faith and works. Are we saved by works or by faith? Ephesians 2:8-10 must be kept together to get the entire picture and when properly understood, they are not in conflict with what we find in other passages, especially the book of James. Let's take a moment to consider this question.

2:8-10

It is important to keep all three of these verses (2:8-10) together when discussing the subject of Faith and Works, or as some say "Faith vs. Works."

Verses 8 and 9 are very familiar and often quoted. The message is clear. We are saved through faith, it is not works that save us. No amount of religious activity or zeal can save our souls. Only trusting in the finished work of Christ can save a person.

Verse 10 tells what happens after a person is saved by faith apart from the works of the law. That person now, because he is a changed person with a changed heart, does good works. These are the evidences of a changed heart. So, a person is not saved by works, but when he is saved, the evidence of that salvation will be that he will do good works.

**When you put these two verses together you learn that faith alone saves, but the faith that saves is never alone.**

But doesn't the book of James teach faith without works is dead?

Some have thought that the book of James gives a different message but they misunderstand what James is saying. Here are some of the verses in James Chapter Two that can be confusing:

> "¹⁴ What use is it, my brethren, if someone says he has faith but he has no works? Can that faith save him? ¹⁵ If a brother or sister is without clothing and in need of daily food, ¹⁶ and one of you says to them, "Go in peace, be warmed and be filled," and yet you do not give them what is necessary for their body, what use is that? ¹⁷ Even so faith, if it has no works, is dead, being by itself.
> ¹⁸ But someone may well say, "You have faith and I have works; show me your faith without the works, and I will show you my faith by my works . . .
> ²⁶ For just as the body without the spirit is dead, so also faith without works is dead." (James 2:14-18,26)

On the surface, it appears James is saying the opposite of what Paul said, but that is why verse 10 is so important in Ephesians Two. It completes the picture.

When James tells us that "faith without works is dead," he is not saying salvation comes by works, but what he is saying is exactly what Paul is saying, namely, that if a person has genuine faith then that faith will produce genuine works like a mango tree produces mangoes. Good works are the fruit of true faith. But a person who does not show good works is not a real believer. His faith that doesn't produce works is a dead faith, not real. Good works are the fruit, or evidence, that the faith is real. If there are no good works in a Christians life, then the faith is not real and the person is not a real believer.

## Here is a simple two-point outline.

**Faith Works!**

> 2:8,9 - **FAITH** works! No amount of human effort can save us. Religion does not work, good deeds do not work, being a member of a church does not work; only faith works. Salvation is by faith alone.

> 2:10 - Faith **WORKS**! And genuine faith produces a life that has genuine good works. A real faith does good works, faith works. A genuine faith goes to work because of a love for God and what He has done for us.

And now, after Paul has shown just how lost man is without Christ and then he has shown just how great grace is, he now reveals that this grace is for all people, both Jew and Gentile.

# SECTION 3
## A wall only God could break down. (Ephesians 2:11-22)

This next section of Chapter Two is a long section but it is one theme.

### Key verse- Ephesians 2:19

> "19 So now you Gentiles are no longer strangers and foreigners. You are citizens along with all of God's holy people. You are members of God's family."

Let's read the entire passage. As you read it watch the grace of God in action, like a flood sweeping over the Gentile peoples and bringing them into the family of God. For the first century Jew, this was a stunning revelation!

### Ephesians 2:11-22 (New Living Translation)

> "11 Don't forget that you Gentiles used to be outsiders. You were called "uncircumcised heathens" by the Jews, who were proud of their circumcision, even though it affected only their bodies and not their hearts. 12 In those days you were living apart from Christ. You were excluded from citizenship among the people of Israel, and you did not know the covenant promises God had made to them. You lived in this world without God and without hope. 13 But now you have been united with Christ Jesus. Once you were far away from God, but now you have been brought near to him through the blood of Christ.
> 14 For Christ himself has brought peace to us. He united Jews and Gentiles into one people when, in his own body on the cross, he broke down the wall of hostility that separated

us. [15] He did this by ending the system of law with its commandments and regulations. He made peace between Jews and Gentiles by creating in himself one new people from the two groups. [16] Together as one body, Christ reconciled both groups to God by means of his death on the cross, and our hostility toward each other was put to death.

[17] He brought this Good News of peace to you Gentiles who were far away from him, and peace to the Jews who were near. [18] Now all of us can come to the Father through the same Holy Spirit because of what Christ has done for us. [19] So now you Gentiles are no longer strangers and foreigners. You are citizens along with all of God's holy people. You are members of God's family. [20] Together, we are his house, built on the foundation of the apostles and the prophets. And the cornerstone is Christ Jesus himself. [21] We are carefully joined together in him, becoming a holy temple for the Lord. [22] Through Him you Gentiles are also being made part of this dwelling where God lives by His Spirit."

The first part of Ephesians Chapter Two was about grace, and now we see grace in action. Two groups of undeserving people, Jews and Gentiles, have found grace and peace with God because of what Christ accomplished on the Cross.

This is a long section with many beautiful truths to explore. Instead of going through these verses one at a time I want to deal with the big story found in this entire passage.

Let's begin with the issues that the Jews and Gentiles faced historically, and then we will look at how the work of Christ at Calvary has taken away all that divided them.

## Major barriers separating Jews and Gentiles in the Old Testament.

**1.** The Jews were often prideful as a special, privileged people. A Gentile woman once begged Jesus for some crumbs from His table and acknowledged she was unworthy as a dog. The Jews referred to the Gentiles as pagans, heathens and dogs. (Matthew 15:21-28)

**2.** The nation of Israel had the Temple, a system of moral laws, priests, sacrifices, the Torah, the words of the prophets and circumcision as the seal of being in God's family. They were a people chosen by God over all other peoples to bring about His plan of salvation. Instead of this being a source of thanksgiving it often resulted in pride.

**3.** The Temple during Jesus time had a dividing wall that kept Gentiles from entering the Temple courts where sacrifices for sin were made.

**4.** The blessings of God were evident on the nation of Israel, but Gentiles were cut off and were strangers and foreigners, excluded from the hope of ever knowing the family relationship with God that Israel claimed.

This passage, Ephesians 2:11-21, completely demolishes all of those barriers. The cross of Christ removed all four of these issues separating the two peoples and brought them together as fellow citizens in the Kingdom of God. Today, all believers are the Temple of the Holy Spirit. We are God's kingdom of priests serving Him and now all believers are part of God's family, His special people.

### Ephesians 2:11-21 teaches us how Jesus has removed each of these barriers:

**1.** The Gentiles are presented as fellow members of the family of God. This would have been very welcome news to many in Ephesus since it was primarily a Gentile city. Both Jew and Gentile are special to God, and Jesus' death was equally for all mankind, not just one race.

**2.** The ceremonial law with its priests, sacrifices and feasts were fulfilled when Jesus died and rose again. The ceremonial law in the Old Testament was a giant visual aid showing what was coming. The lambs sacrificed and the blood shed all pointed to the day when the final Lamb of God Himself would take away the sin of the world. When Jesus died, the veil in the Temple was torn from top to bottom signifying that God had opened the way for all men to come directly into His presence. The nation of Israel were the caretakers of the message of salvation which was for all men, and when Christ died and rose again it was all over. The role of the ceremonial law had accomplished what it was established to do. It was no longer needed.

**3.** The dividing wall in the Temple grounds was built by Herod, but God now says it is no more. Gentiles have equal access to God, without prejudice. In AD 70 when Titus destroyed Herod's Temple as Jesus had predicted, that dividing wall was also torn down. The shadow was gone, Christ has come. Now, our bodies are temples of the Holy Spirit, both Jew and Gentile believers.

**4.** Ephesians along with other New Testament passages are clear that all believers are now fellow heirs of the Kingdom of God — no believer is excluded, Jew or Gentile. No believer is a stranger or foreigner to God.

To better appreciate the enormity of Ephesians 2:11-21 it is helpful to remember the story of these two groups. The Jew and Gentile division was a huge issue in the Biblical times. It is helpful to try to put ourselves back in that time when we read this passage.

## Historical Insight
### A brief history of the Jews and Gentiles.

## The story of mankind.

God created the world and mankind. Man fell into sin and the curse that resulted impacted all of humanity and even the entire created universe (Romans 8). But God, who is rich in mercy, had a rescue plan for His creation from the beginning (Genesis 3:15). Mankind populated the world, but the sin of man became great on the earth so God destroyed the world by a flood saving only Noah and his family (Genesis 8-10).

## The story of Israel.

The entire human race today has descended from the three sons of Noah whose names were Ham, Shem and Japheth.

> *"The sons of Japheth became the peoples mentioned in Genesis 10:2-5, settling in Asia Minor, Greece, Russia, Cyprus, and Southeastern Europe.*
>
> *The sons of Ham, mentioned in Genesis 10:6-20, mostly inhabited much of Asia and lived in Southern Europe and Northern Africa. They were the original inhabitants of the land that God later gave to Israel.*
>
> *The sons of Shem, mentioned in Genesis 10:21-31, in general, occupied the Middle East. Important to the Bible is the fact that the descendants of Shem included Abraham and Israel and also Jesus Christ."* (John F. Walvoord)

God in His sovereignty chose a particular people to accomplish his rescue plan for the entire human race. He picked Abraham from the line of Shem to become the father of that chosen race. They were not called chosen because they were special, but because God sovereignly chose them. Abraham, Isaac and Jacob became the beginning of a new people and God made a covenant with them and promised to bless the entire earth through the children of Abraham (Genesis 12:1-3). Jacob was given a new name, Israel, and the

Jewish nation began. They had a divinely appointed purpose in the plan of God.

> "⁴ They are the people of Israel, chosen to be God's adopted children, God revealed his glory to them. He made covenants with them and gave them his law. He gave them the privilege of worshiping him and receiving his wonderful promises. ⁵ Abraham, Isaac, and Jacob are their ancestors, and Christ himself was an Israelite as far as his human nature is concerned. And he is God, the one who rules over everything and is worthy of eternal praise! Amen."
> (Romans 9:4-5)

Israel was not always faithful as the channel of God's divine revelation to the world but God still accomplished his plan through them.

> "⁴But when the right time came, God sent his Son, born of a woman, subject to the law. ⁵ God sent him to buy freedom for us who were slaves to the law, so that he could adopt us as his very own children." (Galatians 4:4,5)

## The story of the Gentiles.

Nations that are not Jewish are called "Goyim" in Scripture. That word is commonly translated in various versions of the Bible as "nations" or "Gentiles" and sometimes as "heathen." Even so, the Gentile nations were not hated or despised and even enjoyed the hospitality of the Israelites who were commanded to love them (Deut. 10:19). Many Gentile people have significant roles in Biblical history like Rahab, Uriah the Hittite, Ruth, and others. When Solomon dedicated the Jewish Temple in Jerusalem he prayed as follows:

> "⁴¹In the future, foreigners who do not belong to your people Israel will hear of you. They will come from distant lands because of your name, ⁴² for they will hear of your great name and your strong hand and your powerful arm.

And when they pray toward this Temple, [43] then hear from heaven where you live, and grant what they ask of you. In this way, all the people of the earth will come to know and fear you, just as your own people Israel do. They, too, will know that this Temple I have built honors your name." (1 Kings 8:41-43)

## Race and Grace - God has always been an all-peoples' God.

From the first page of Genesis to the last words of Revelation, it is clear that God has always been there for all the people of the world. Jesus is the lamb of God that takes away the sins of the world, not just the Jewish world. God has always shown mercy on all who call upon His Name.

But the nation of Israel often lost sight of God's love for all people and became arrogant, referring to the gentiles as sinners. Paul, in Romans Chapters 1-3, spends a lot of time showing that the Gentiles are sinners, the Jews are sinners and then all are sinners and fall short of the Glory of God.

The level of arrogance of the Jews concerning their race and heritage was revealed when Herod rebuilt the temple in Jerusalem. A feature was added that had not been seen in Solomon's or Zerubbabel's rebuilt temple. Herod expanded the larger court areas outside the temple, but at the insistence of the Jews, he added a large middle wall that cut off the inner courts from the large outer court. This wall of partition made a new section, called the court of the Gentiles. No Gentile was allowed to cross beyond that barricade under penalty of death. They could participate as a worshiper from a distance and were allowed to be believers, but they were always considered uncircumcised and outsiders of the nation, or commonwealth of Israel. This is the wall mentioned in verse 14.

"[13] But now in Christ Jesus you who formerly were far off have been brought near by the blood of Christ. [14] For He

Himself is our peace, who made both groups into one and broke down the <u>barrier of the dividing wall</u>,"
(New American Standard Bible, Ephesians 2:13, 14, emphasis mine)

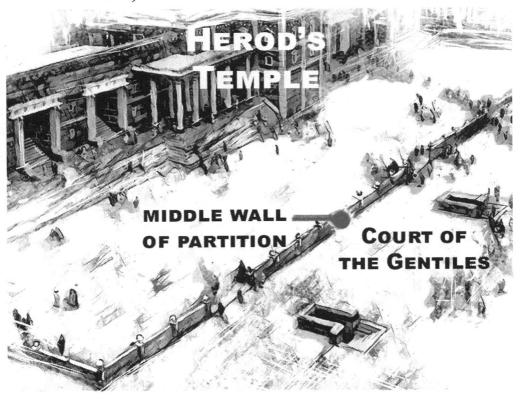

HEROD'S TEMPLE

MIDDLE WALL OF PARTITION

COURT OF THE GENTILES

"For there is no distinction between Jew and Greek; for the same Lord is Lord of all, abounding in riches for all who call upon Him; for 'Whoever will call upon the name of the Lord will be saved' " (Romans 10:12-13)

## Summary of Chapter Two

Ephesians Chapter Two is a flood of grace pouring over the entire world as well as over that wall. For all who travel through the dry desert of sin containing only dead, deceived, depraved and doomed souls comes the life-giving water of God. Yes, no matter how desperate the condition and how deep the darkness, God's love and grace are deeper. No matter how great the divide and prejudices between Jew and Gentile, God has broken down every barrier and made one new family, His forever family.  What grace. What a God we have!

# Ephesians Chapter Three

# MYSTERY

## Overview

Chapter one was primarily about God. Chapter Two is about grace. Chapter Three takes us deeper into both grace and the greatness of God as it reveals a mystery which was never known before the New Testament times. It is the mystery of Christ and the Church, a church made up of all believing Jew and Gentile people.

Can you imagine what it would have been like to have God whisper in your ear and tell you something that was never known since the beginning of the world? It happened to Paul, and now we all get to hear about it. A great mystery has now been revealed.

Ephesians Chapter Three is basically about two things. The first section is about this great mystery, and the other thing is the second prayer Paul prays for the Ephesian believers.

# Outline

Here are two suggested messages that give an overview of Chapter Three:

**Section 1** | (Ephesians 3:1-13)
Secrets and mysteries revealed.

**Section 2** | (Ephesians 3:14-21)
How to pray for one another in the church.
(Paul's second prayer for the believers in Ephesus.)

# Commentary

## SECTION 1
### Secrets and mysteries revealed.

Ephesians 3:1-13

"For this reason, I, Paul, the prisoner of Christ Jesus for
the sake of you Gentiles— ²if indeed you have heard of the
stewardship of God's grace which was given to me for you;
³that by revelation there was made known to me the mystery, as I wrote before in brief. ⁴By referring to this, when
you read you can understand my insight into the mystery
of Christ, ⁵which in other generations was not made known
to the sons of men, as it has now been revealed to His holy
apostles and prophets in the Spirit; ⁶to be specific, that the
Gentiles are fellow heirs and fellow members of the body,
and fellow partakers of the promise in Christ Jesus through
the gospel, ⁷of which I was made a minister, according to
the gift of God's grace which was given to me according
to the working of His power. ⁸To me, the very least of all
saints, this grace was given, to preach to the Gentiles the
unfathomable riches of Christ, ⁹and to bring to light what is
the administration of the mystery which for ages has been
hidden in God who created all things; ¹⁰so that the man-
ifold wisdom of God might now be made known through
the church to the rulers and the authorities in the heavenly
places. ¹¹This was in accordance with the eternal purpose
which He carried out in Christ Jesus our Lord, ¹²in whom we
have boldness and confident access through faith in Him.
¹³Therefore I ask you not to lose heart at my tribulations on
your behalf, for they are your glory." (Ephesians 3:1-13)

## Important note:

There are many fine commentaries written on the book of Ephesians, and many of them go verse by verse through the book, some even doing lengthy discussions about each word used. The purpose of this commentary is to help the reader understand the big messages of the book. Once a person grasps the bigger picture then the small details make more sense. I will leave the small details to other writers and to your personal study. I want you to see the flow of the book and the large themes of this amazing letter.

## Background information on mysteries in the Bible.

When we think of the word "mystery," we tend to think about an unsolved crime or an event we can't explain. Once we solve the mystery, it is no longer a mystery. The Bible uses both of these types of meanings, things we cannot understand and others that were hidden at one time but now have been revealed.

There are many mysteries in life and there will always be unanswered questions. The greatest of all mysteries concern God.

> **"Can you search out the deep things of God?**
> **Can you find out the limits of the Almighty?**
> **They are higher than heaven— what can you do?**
> **Deeper than Sheol— what can you know?"** (Job 11:7-8)

God is infinite in power, knowledge, love and every one of His unfathomable attributes. As believers, we will be amazed every second of eternity with something new we learn about God. It will be a continuous and thrilling, never-ending discovery.

**Let's briefly look at three types of mysteries we find in God's Word:**

## Category One.

There are some things that God knows that He never tells anybody because we are not able to understand them, or for reasons known only to God.

They remain God's secrets alone:

> **"The secret things belong unto the Lord our God, but the things that are revealed belong unto us and our children forever."** (Deuteronomy 29:29)

Our little brains could never conceive of all the grandeur of God's knowledge. There are some things He cannot tell us yet. When our children were small we didn't allow them to do certain things like playing in the street or running around with sharp objects. We could not explain to them at that time why, so we just enforced our rules to protect them.

## Category Two.

God has some secrets that He only reveals to His children. These are family secrets.

> **"The secret of the Lord is with them that fear Him. And He will show them His covenant."** (Psalm 25:14)

> **"His secret is with the righteous."** (Proverbs 3:32)

> **"He reveals His secrets unto His servants."** (Amos 3:7)

The parables of Jesus show us that we know things the unsaved don't know.

> **"[25] At that time Jesus said, "I praise You, Father, Lord of heaven and earth, that You have hidden these things from the wise and intelligent and have revealed them to infants. [26] Yes, Father, for this way was well-pleasing in Your sight.**

**27** All things have been handed over to Me by My Father; and no one knows the Son except the Father; nor does anyone know the Father except the Son, and anyone to whom the Son wills to reveal Him." (Matthew 11:25-27)

"...the disciples came and said to Him, 'Why do You speak to them in parables?' He answered and said to them, 'Because it has been given to you to know the mysteries of the kingdom of heaven, but to them it has not been given.'" (Matthew 13:10-11)

## Category Three.

There are some things which God kept secret from everybody for a period of time and finally revealed them to the church through His special servants in the New Testament. The book of Daniel tells how God, who revealed mysteries to His prophet in the Old Testament, kept back certain other mysteries until a later time.

"**8** As for me, I heard but could not understand; so I said, "My lord, what will be the outcome of these events?" **9** He said, "Go your way, Daniel, for these words are concealed and sealed up until the end time. **10** Many will be purged, purified and refined, but the wicked will act wickedly; and none of the wicked will understand, but those who have insight will understand." (Daniel 12:8-10)

In the book of Ephesians and other New Testament books we are privileged to understand some of the mysteries that the ancient prophets didn't understand. Paul writes:

"**25** I have become its servant by the commission God gave me to present to you the word of God in its fullness— **26** the mystery that has been kept hidden for ages and generations, but is now disclosed to the Lord's people. **27** To them God has chosen to make known among the Gentiles the glorious riches of this mystery, which is Christ in you, the hope of glory." (Colossians 1:25-27)

Ephesians reveals the great mysteries of the gospel and the church.

This third usage is what Paul is referring to when he describes the *"mystērion"* of the Church, made up of both Jews and Gentiles.

The Greek word *"mystērion"* *according to Greek lexicons generally refers to:*

> "A hidden purpose or counsel of God: the secret counsels which govern God in dealing with the righteous, which are hidden from ungodly and wicked men but plain to the godly."

Each of the first three chapters of Ephesians make reference to this mystery: 1:9-12, 2:11, 12 and 3:3-13.

## So, what is the mystery of the Church?

The answer is clearly stated in Ephesians 3:2-6.

> "2 if indeed you have heard of the stewardship of God's grace which was given to me for you; 3 that by revelation there was made known to me the mystery, as I wrote before in brief. 4 By referring to this, when you read you can understand my insight into <u>the mystery of Christ</u>, 5 which in other generations was not made known to the sons of men, as it has now been revealed to His holy apostles and prophets in the Spirit; 6 to be specific, that the Gentiles are fellow heirs and fellow members of the body, and fellow partakers of the promise in Christ Jesus through the gospel."
> (Ephesians 3:2-6, emphasis mine)

Maybe you are thinking, what is so mysterious about this? We all know that God loves all people. We know that God is color blind; He does not elevate one race over another. He does not play favorites. All believers are equal as children in His family, whether male or female, bond or free, Jew or Gentile. The Lamb of God takes away the sin of the world and one day every nation, tribe, people and language will be represented before the throne and worship Him (Revelation 7:9). He is the all-peoples' God.

But this passage in Ephesians is clear that these things we know today and often take for granted were not known until God revealed them to his apostles in the first century.

> "[6] to be specific, that the Gentiles are fellow heirs and fellow members of the body, and fellow partakers of the promise in Christ Jesus through the gospel, [7] of which I was made a minister, according to the gift of God's grace which was given to me according to the working of His power. [8] To me, the very least of all saints, this grace was given, to preach to the Gentiles the unfathomable riches of Christ, [9] and to bring to light what is the administration of the mystery which for ages has been hidden in God who created all things; [10] so that the manifold wisdom of God might now be made known through the church to the rulers and the authorities in the heavenly places. [11] This was in accordance with the eternal purpose which He carried out in Christ Jesus our Lord, [12] in whom we have boldness and confident access through faith in Him. [13] Therefore I ask you not to lose heart at my tribulations on your behalf, for they are your glory."

## An interesting word.

There is a Greek word Paul uses three times in Ephesians. It is the word, "*Oikonomia.*" It is where we get the English word "Economy." Here are the three verses:

> Ephesians 1:10
> "with a view to an administration *(Oikonomia)* suitable to the fullness of the times, that is, the summing up of all things in Christ, things in the heavens and things on the earth. . ."

> Ephesians 3:2
> "if indeed you have heard of the stewardship *(Oikonomia)* of God's grace which was given to me for you;"

Ephesians 3:9

**"and to bring to light what is the administration** *(Oikonomia)* **of the mystery which for ages has been hidden in God who created all things;"**

The word *"Oikonomia" is* often translated economy, steward-ship, management and dispensation. If you have ever heard of the word dispensation or dispensational theology it comes from this word. The word is really about management. Think of a person who works for a company and is appointed as a manager. It is that person's role, or responsibility to make sure the wishes of the own-er are carried out and the purposes of the company are achieved. The manager has a responsibility to make sure the company vision or plans are carried out properly.

This is what Paul is referring to. He understood that God had given him an insight, an understanding into a great mystery that had not been known before. And God had made him a manager, a responsi-ble steward to make sure that the church would understand what God was doing. In Ephesians, Paul is performing his God-assigned role and telling the church then and today that both Jew and Gen-tile are joint heirs with Christ. All believers, Jew and Gentile, are one body in Christ. Paul was given the keys and understanding to unlock this great mystery in the past, something only God knew, and now we are all privileged to understand it.

## Questions.

- Why did God wait so long?
- Why did He keep it hidden from even his greatest prophets in the Old Testament?
- Why was the Apostle Paul given special insight into this mys-tery that others before him never understood?

Paul himself seems amazed in this passage that he, the least of the apostles, was given this special grace to be the one to reveal this plan of God to the church. God is sovereign in all He does. He chooses the seasons and the people. He is God, Lord over all. Paul marveled that he was picked and this was the time God had chosen to reveal what had been hidden in Him since the foundation of the earth. This is the only answer to the questions about why God waited. He waited because He is God, and He had a plan and chose to wait. He alone determines the times and the seasons. What a privilege for us today to understand these things and to be children of our amazing and unfathomable God.

## One final thought on this section.

Verses 10 and 11 reveal something else about God and the church. They reveal what God's primary purpose is for the church, the reason for its existence.

> "**[10] so that the manifold wisdom of God might now be made known through the church to the rulers and the authorities in the heavenly places. [11] This was in accordance with the eternal purpose which He carried out in Christ Jesus our Lord,**" (Ephesians 3:10-11)

More than a few passages in the Bible teach us that all we do is ultimately for the glory of God. Everything God has ever done, everything He has ever made was made to bring glory to Himself. If man tries to bring glory to himself it is sin, but when God brings glory to Himself it is His rightful nature. Ephesians 3:10 and 11 tell us that the church, made of Jew and Gentile believers, united in Christ, is a testimony to the entire angelic realm, good angels and fallen angels.

The church proclaims the wisdom and greatness of His purpose and glorifies Him as the one and only true God. To the fallen angelic world, the church stands as a clear testimony to the eternal wisdom of God and a condemnation of their rebellion against God. They were powerless to stop the birth of the Son of God and could not keep Him in the tomb. They were unable to stop the church and they will not be able to stop their final judgment. The church by its existence proclaims throughout the universe that a God of wisdom, grace and holiness is in charge and He alone is worthy of worship.

## SECTION 2
## How to pray for one another in the Church.

### Ephesians 3:14-21

The first section of Chapter Three was about the mystery of the church. The second main section of Ephesians Chapter Three is Paul's second prayer for the Ephesian believers. His first prayer was given after that amazing passage in Ephesians 1:3-14 where God reveals many things about Himself. Paul prays that the church would receive enlightenment from God so they could better understand the things God had just revealed.

The second prayer follows two chapters which teach us that while we were desperate sinners, God by his grace has changed us into a unified church made up of both Jew and Gentile. We are now the church of God and bring glory to God in heaven and on earth. God now holds us up as His masterpiece proclaiming his glory before the angels and demons. He is God. He is Good, and we are His family.

Paul now prays his second prayer for the church that we will be empowered by God to live out our lives as victorious believers lifting up the reputation of God. Paul's prayer will show us that the power to live this out comes from God Himself, who is unlimited in power. Let's read that prayer.

**Paul's first prayer was for enlightenment and his second is for empowerment.**

"¹⁴ For this reason I bow my knees before the Father, ¹⁵ from whom every family in heaven and on earth derives its name, ¹⁶ that He would grant you, according to the riches of His glory, to be strengthened with power through His Spirit in the inner man, ¹⁷ so that Christ may dwell in your hearts through faith; and that you, being rooted and grounded in love, ¹⁸ may be able to comprehend with all the saints what is the breadth and length and height and depth, ¹⁹ and to know the love of Christ which surpasses knowledge, that you may be filled up to all the fullness of God.
²⁰ Now to Him who is able to do far more abundantly beyond all that we ask or think, according to the power that works within us, ²¹ to Him be the glory in the church and in Christ Jesus to all generations forever and ever. Amen."
(Ephesians 3:14-21)

Up to this point we have seen in the first three chapters just how great God is, how sinful man is and we have explored the incredible church that God has assembled with both Jew and Gentile. Now, the rest of the book of Ephesians will be about living the Christian life. It is one thing to believe all the right things but another thing to live that life out. The foundations have been laid in Chapters One through Three and now it is time to move from knowing about Christ and His Church to living like Christians. But in our own strength we will fail. We need God's strength and His power in our lives. That is what Paul prays for in verses 14-21.

## Ephesians 3:14-17
**Paul's prayer is addressed to the triune God.**

### Ephesians 3:14-15 - The Father.
God the Father is acknowledged as the source of the human race, and just as a human father is the head of a human family, God is the Head of the human race and specifically the church family. No matter what tribe, tongue or people, we all, as the body of Christ, have one Father, God.

### Ephesians 3:16 - The Holy Spirit.

He is the one sent to us to strengthen us. He comes to strengthen us with all His power and glory. His desire is to make us strong to withstand the enemy of our souls. His plan is to have us walk as victorious believers in a hostile world. The last three chapters of Ephesians will detail what that walk looks like. But before Paul gets to that, he wants to be sure that we are ready for it. We need to be equipped to live out what he is about to tell us. We need the filling and leading and teaching of the Holy Spirit to do that.

### Ephesians 3:17 - Jesus Christ, the Son of God.

Our Lord is then invited to dwell in our hearts through faith. The picture is a great tree that has deep roots in solid ground. We are like that tree when we are fully trusting our Savior. We can withstand any storm and attack. Our roots grow deep in the very love of God.

## Easter Heights.

Years ago, as a missionary in the Philippines, I noticed a new subdivision of homes being built in the foothills outside Manila. The view was beautiful. The subdivision was called Easter Heights. Its motto was "Living above it all." That may be a good illustration of what the primary purpose of this prayer is all about. God knows that for us to live in victory, to live above it all, we need God's strength, not our own strength. Jesus faced every temptation we do, He suffered for each of our sins and He died so we don't have to face the eternal punishment we deserve. He then rose victoriously and defeated the armies of Hell on that great Easter morning. Now He wants us to live in His resurrection power, His "Easter Heights." He wants us to live above it all.

What would a life be like that was fully surrendered to God? What would it be like to be always filled with the Holy Spirit of understanding, indwelt by the living Son of God and having His heart of love in our hearts?  It would be a life that would be best described in the next two verses:

## Ephesians 3:18-19

> ". . . that we may be able to comprehend with all the saints what is the breadth and length and height and depth, [19] and to know the love of Christ which surpasses knowledge, that you may be filled up to all the fullness of God."

This entire prayer is like the ending of the Hallelujah Chorus. It builds and builds until we are caught up in worship, like we are pulled into the very throne room of God.  The last two verses in this prayer ends the chapter with a great crescendo.

## Ephesians 3:20-21

> "[20] Now unto him that is able to do exceeding abundantly above all that we ask or think, according to the power that worketh in us, [21] Unto him be glory in the church by Christ Jesus throughout all ages, world without end. Amen."
> (King James Version)

### How is your imagination?

Before we take a look at these verses I want you to try to imagine something. What if God told you that anything you can imagine or think up for what Heaven would be like, He would do. Anything at all.  Let your imagination soar.  What incredible thing can you come up with?  Just go along with me for a moment and do it.

OK, here is a thought I had. What if I took the most wonderful moment in all my life, the most joyful, most peaceful experience and I asked God to double that joy and double it again and again every second and to keep doubling it every second forever.  Could God do that? He is infinitely powerful and unlimited. Yes, He could do that. But that is not what God is going to do. What he is going to do is much more than that. Verse. 20 says we have a God who can do:

**Exceeding**
**Abundantly**
**Above**
**All we could ask or ever think**

Let's start with the best we can think of, all we can ask or think. He can do that. But He can do beyond or above all we can ask or think. But there is more, He can do abundantly, beyond all we can ask or think. But there is more. He can do exceeding, abundantly beyond all we can ask or think. I hope you are getting excited about what is coming for His children. But these verses aren't just about what is coming in eternity, they are a statement that the God who fills us with His Spirit in this life and strengthens us is that same God who will help us in ways we can't even imagine when we surrender to Him. When we call on Him, He is able to do Exceeding Abundantly, Above, All we could ever ask or think! As an old preacher once said, "If that doesn't light your fire, your wood is wet!"

## Summary of Chapter Three

In Chapter One Paul prayed that the Ephesian believers would be enlightened, that the eyes of their understanding would learn more deeply about God. Then in Chapter Three, Paul prays that God would empower their lives and equip them to walk in a manner worthy of their great calling, and He promises His infinite power and love would fill theirs and our lives to live in a way that will glorify Him.

The next logical thing for Paul to tell us what God expects from His church. What kinds of lives does He want us to live? That is exactly what we learn in Ephesians Chapters Four through Six.

# Ephesians Chapter Four

## God's Community

## Overview

If we had to briefly summarize the first three chapters of Ephesians, we could say it is about our amazing God and the grace He has shown to such a fallen people. He has not only saved us but has changed us and formed us into a unified church made up of Jew and Gentile. This church now stands as a lighthouse to the world. It proclaims the wisdom of our Creator to everyone including angels and demons. By Grace we are God's chosen children to be ambassadors of His Kingdom, citizens of the community of God.

The next thee chapters are instructions about practical Christian living in a fallen and dark world. Chapter Four will be broken into four topics or sections.

# Outline

**SECTION 1** | Ephesians 4:1-6
Unity in the body of Christ.

**SECTION 2** | Ephesians 4:7-10
What happened when Jesus died?

**Section 3** | Ephesians 4:11-16
The leadership and purpose of the church.

> 4:11, 12 - The Church leadership established by God.
> 4:12-16 - Godly leaders build mature churches.

**SECTION 4** | Ephesians 4:17-32
The life we are called to lead as Christians.

> 4:17-19 – The beauty of truth and understanding. contrasted with the error and darkness of the lost.

> 4:20-24 – A call to God's higher standard.

> 4:25-32 – Practical instructions for believers.

## Important background.

Chapter Four begins with a topic very important to the Apostle Paul. He had spent 18 months establishing the church in Corinth, but the believers were really not getting along well. While in Ephesus, Paul wrote his first of two letters to them. The entire epistle of 1 Corinthians is a letter of rebuke over a number of serious sins. Here is some of what he wrote to them:

> **"10 Now I exhort you, brethren, by the name of our Lord Jesus Christ, that you all agree and that there be no divisions among you, but that you be made complete in the same mind and in the same judgment. 11 For I have been informed concerning you, my brethren, by Chloe's people, that there are quarrels among you. 12 Now I mean this, that each one of you is saying, "I am of Paul," and "I of Apollos," and "I of Cephas," and "I of Christ."** (1 Corinthians 1:10-12)

The first problem Paul dealt with in 1 Corinthians, the issue of lack of unity in the church, is the same topic he begins with in Chapter Four of Ephesians, the issue of unity within the body.

# Commentary

## SECTION 1
## Unity in the body of Christ. (Ephesians 4:1-6)

> "Therefore I, the prisoner of the Lord, implore you to walk in a manner worthy of the calling with which you have been called, ² with all humility and gentleness, with patience, showing tolerance for one another in love, ³ being diligent to preserve the unity of the Spirit in the bond of peace. ⁴ There is one body and one Spirit, just as also you were called in one hope of your calling; ⁵ one Lord, one faith, one baptism, ⁶ one God and Father of all who is over all and through all and in all."

Just before we discuss what unity is all about. It is helpful to remind ourselves what Jesus said about it when he prayed for His disciples just before he went to the cross.

> "²⁰ I do not ask on behalf of these alone, but for those also who believe in Me through their word; ²¹that they may all be one; even as You, Father, are in Me and I in You, that they also may be in Us, so that the world may believe that You sent Me. ²² The glory which You have given Me I have given to them, that they may be one, just as We are one; ²³ I in them and You in Me, that they may be perfected in unity, so that the world may know that You sent Me, and loved them, even as You have loved Me." (John 17:20-23)

Sometimes people think that just because they meet together for a worship service and greet one another that they are unified. Just because we are together (union) does not mean we are showing loving concern, forgiving attitudes and humble tolerant spirits to one another with the goal of building each other up (unity). If I took two cats and tied their tails together and hung them over a fence that would be union, but it would not be unity!

### Ephesians 4:1-3 - What unity means.

> **"Therefore I, the prisoner of the Lord, implore you to walk in a manner worthy of the calling with which you have been called, [2] with all humility and gentleness, with patience, showing tolerance for one another in love, [3] being diligent to preserve the unity of the Spirit in the bond of peace."**

If we list the character qualities found in these three verses it is like a blueprint for church unity. We each need to take that blueprint and apply these spiritual disciplines into our lives:

- We need humility (not arrogance or boasting).
- We need to be gentle towards each other (not rudeness).
- We need patience with each other (not demanding).
- We need tolerance for each other's differences (not judgmental).
- We need to love one another (not selfish or self-centered).
- We need to be peacemakers (not one who argues).

Does that list sound familiar?

> **"But the fruit of the Spirit is love, joy, peace, patience, kindness, goodness, faithfulness, [23] gentleness, self-control; against such things there is no law."**
> (Galatians 5:22,23)

A church composed of members who demonstrate the fruits of the Holy Spirit is a church that will have unity. When we walk with God, we will walk with each other.

But does this mean we will always agree with each other on everything? Of course not, but even when we disagree we can still be kind, gentle, tolerant, etc. Paul does list, however, seven things where the church should be in general agreement. These seven foundational teachings are a bond, a spiritual glue which help hold us together. To live in community, we need common unity.

## Ephesians 4:4-6 - Seven things that should unify the church, not divide it.

> "**4 There is one body and one Spirit, just as also you were called in one hope of your calling; 5 one Lord, one faith, one baptism, 6 one God and Father of all who is over all and through all and in all."**

An army may be made up of different kinds of people, but when they are committed to a common purpose, they can win a war by working together.

We are in a spiritual war (more about this war when we get to Chapter Six), and as soldiers of God we need to not only know our enemy but commit to support each other. We also are to protect each other and focus our energy on the enemy, not against each other. We all know that at times that is easy to say but hard to do.

> *"To live above with saints we love, Oh, won't that be glory! But, to live below with saints we know, now that's another story!" (Unknown author)*

So, let's look at these seven foundational truths where God wants us to stand together.

## 1 - There is one body.

Remember the problem in Corinth when the people were saying, "I am of Paul," and "I of Apollos," and "I of Cephas," and "I of Christ."

Our version of that today is I go to this church or that one, or my denomination is right, or we believe we are the true church. Maybe we boast in a particular preacher or we exclude others who don't use a particular version of the Bible. There are many ways we can be intolerant of others within the body of Christ.

> **"12 The human body has many parts, but the many parts make up one whole body. So it is with the body of Christ. 13 Some of us are Jews, some are Gentiles, some are slaves, and some are free. But we have all been baptized into one body by one Spirit, and we all share the same Spirit."**
> (1 Corinthians 12:12.13)

God tells us that all believers make up His one body. Then He pleads with us to act like it.

## 2 - There is one Spirit.

Ephesus was a pagan city with temples and priests teaching false religions. There were many voices and lying spirits. Paul was making sure the believers recognized the true Spirit in their lives, the Spirit of the living God. Maybe Paul was particularly careful in helping the believers in Ephesus understand who the Holy Spirit is because they had little understanding at all of the Scriptures or the Spirit of God when he first spent time with them.

> **"While Apollos was at Corinth, Paul took the road through the interior and arrived at Ephesus. There he found some disciples 2 and asked them, "Did you receive the Holy Spirit when you believed?" They answered, "No, we have not even heard that there is a Holy Spirit."** (Acts 19:1.2)

We learn more about the Holy Spirit from the book of Ephesians than from any other single book in the Bible.

1:13) The Spirit seals every believer in Christ, stamps His ownership on our hearts.

4:30) Our sealing is unto the day of redemption and the Holy Spirit of God is our guarantee of salvation.

2:18) It is the Holy Spirit who gives us access to the Father. He is the key to the throne room of the Father.

2:22) We see that the Holy Spirit indwells every believer on earth.

3:5) The Holy Spirit reveals the deep things of God, particularly the mystery of the church. He is our teacher.

3:16) He strengthens every believer.

4:3) He is the bonding agent of all believers. He is the One that holds us together as a body.

4:30) This verse teaches us that the Holy Spirit is a person, He can be grieved.

5:18) We learn that every believer is to submit to the one Holy Spirit all the time.

6:17) The weapon of His warfare is the Word of God.

6:18) He enables the believer to pray. There is no prayer apart from the Holy Spirit.

We have one body, and that one body is indwelt by one Spirit. We don't just have one Spirit, but we have the *One and Only*, the Holy Spirit Himself!

**Leader Notes**

The fact that the Holy Spirit can be grieved proves He is a person, not a force. You can't grieve a radar beam or gravity. You can only grieve a person. But this verse reminds us that there are other sins against the Holy Spirit, and that would be a helpful lesson or message. Here is an outline that might be helpful:

## SINS AGAINST THE HOLY SPIRIT

**It is possible to blaspheme (speak against) the Holy Spirit.** (Matthew 12:31-32, Mark 3:28,29)

**It is possible to insult the Holy Spirit.**
(Hebrews 10:26-29)

**It is possible to put out the Spirit's fire, quench His activity.** (1 Thessalonians 5:19)

**It is possible to grieve the Holy Spirit, injure His person.** (Ephesians 4:25)

**It is possible to lie to and to tempt the Holy Spirit.**
(Acts 5:3-9)

**It is possible to resist the Holy Spirit.** (Acts 7:51)

**It is possible to rebel against the Holy Spirit.**
(Psalm 106:33)

**It is possible to profane the Holy Spirit.**
(1 Corinthians 6:19)

## 3 - There is one hope.

> "... so that, having been justified by his grace, we might become heirs having the hope of eternal life." (Titus 3:7)

The believers in Ephesus walked daily in streets and marketplaces where idols were sold. They lived in a world of pagan temples and immoral practices. It was a world of darkness. The large library in

4:4-6

the city boasted a variety of writings of the philosophers, people trying to make sense out of the world. Immortality was a common theme in Greek mythology but there was no guarantee for the people. Their gods were frail and flawed and often at war with each other. It was all hopeless confusion and ultimately devoid of hope.

> "⁹ How foolish are those who manufacture idols.
>     These prized objects are really worthless.
> The people who worship idols don't know this,
>     so they are all put to shame.
> ¹⁰ Who but a fool would make his own god—
>     an idol that cannot help him one bit?
> ¹¹ All who worship idols will be disgraced
>     along with all these craftsmen—mere humans—
>     who claim they can make a god.
> They may all stand together,
>     but they will stand in terror and shame." (Isaiah 44:9-11)

But it was different for the believers in Ephesus. The Lord God Almighty is the One and only true God, and He alone offers the one and only true hope for mankind. Real hope is found in our real God, not stone statues or empty philosophy. The entire body of Christ shares the one hope of eternity with Him and all the promises that go along with it. For those in Ephesus, who were raised in pagan practices, the message is that Christianity is not Jesus plus other gods, it is just Jesus, our one and only hope of eternal life.

## 4 - There is one Lord.

The uniqueness of Jesus cannot be disputed. No other religion in the world tells of the Creator of the universe becoming flesh to live a perfect life, die on a cross as our substitute for sin and rise from the dead. No other religious founder or leader would dare state that they were God, but Jesus was clear on that issue. Most religions provide gurus, teachers, shamans, or holy men to show their followers what path they need to take to earn their salvation or the right to become part of a big nothing. But in Christianity alone we understand that sin is the issue, not our environment. In Christ alone we have forgiveness, something neither Zeus or Aphrodite nor any other false god could offer. Paul is reminding the Ephesian believers of their unique Savior, their unique hope and a future sealed in the blood of the Lamb. There is only one Lord and savior.

## 5 - There is one faith.

Before Paul came to Ephesus for his three-year ministry in that great city, he had been in Athens, Greece and then in Corinth. In Athens, he stood before the learned religious leaders and philosophers on Mars Hill and presented Jesus to them. They took pride in keeping informed about every new idea and philosophy and belief. But what they heard that day was different and some were drawn to the One who died on the cross and rose from the dead. The story Paul told that day was very different from what they heard before. This was not just a story of a new god, a new teacher, a new idea. This was not just a new way for man to walk to find peace; this was about a faith that changes a life and offers eternal life.

When Paul moved on from Corinth, he went to a similar type of environment in Ephesus with pagan Greek and Roman temples and a wide variety of philosophies and beliefs. But his message was the same, "By grace are you saved by faith." And all believers are brought into the family of God by that same faith and are unified in common hope and the common truth that "there is no other name under Heaven whereby we are saved." Not only is a man saved by faith but our faith is based on the revealed word of God. Of all the voices that cry out to us there is only one voice we need to listen to, the voice of the Living God found in His word. That is our one common faith.

> "Dear friends, although I was very eager to write to you
> about the salvation we share, I felt compelled to write and

4:4-6

urge you to contend for the faith that was once for all entrusted to God's holy people." (Jude 3)

## 6 - There is one baptism.

Some of the first people Paul met when he returned to Ephesus were a group of new disciples. He found out they had not heard of the Holy Spirit. He then asked them if they had been baptized.

So Paul asked,

> "Then what baptism did you receive?"
> "John's baptism," they replied.
> [4] Paul said, "John's baptism was a baptism of repentance. He told the people to believe in the one coming after him, that is, in Jesus." [5] On hearing this, they were baptized in the name of the Lord Jesus." (Acts 19:3,4)

These early disciples, probably the first converts in Ephesus, were brought to faith by a believer named Apollos. This had happened before Paul arrived in Ephesus.

> "[24] Meanwhile a Jew named Apollos, a native of Alexandria, came to Ephesus. He was a learned man, with a thorough knowledge of the Scriptures. [25] He had been instructed in the way of the Lord, and he spoke with great fervor and taught about Jesus accurately, though he knew only the baptism of John." (Acts 18:24,25)

Everything was still in the infancy stage. Apollos under the training of Aquilla and Priscilla and the apostle Paul would become a great and powerful preacher of the Gospel over the entire region. But at this time in history when Paul arrived, he found that the current small band of believers had a limited knowledge of the things of God, especially about the Holy Spirit and believer's baptism.

Some people hold different views on what "one baptism" means. Some say it means water baptism and others say baptism of the

Spirit. It is probably a larger picture in view rather than just one or the other. Paul wrote to Corinth that all believers are "baptized by one Spirit into the body." That is the work of the Holy Spirit at salvation for all believers. The Spirit of God places us in the body of Christ, or immerses us, so to speak, spiritually into the church, the family of God. We are born of the spirit (John 3:3-8) and then we are *"all baptized by one Spirit so as to form one body—whether Jews or Gentiles, slave or free—and we were all given the one Spirit to drink."* (1 Corinthians 12:13)

After a believer has been born again then water baptism is the way he outwardly proclaims to the world what has happened inwardly. That is why immersion is the best way to outwardly demonstrate to others what the Holy Spirit has done inwardly by immersing him into the body of Christ. Water baptism is like putting on a team uniform and proclaiming, "I am on God's team!"

It is most likely that the one baptism in this passage is referring to the entire event, the inward work of the Holy Spirit and the outward testimony of water baptism. It is one unique event that is only found in the Christian church and uniquely sets us apart as followers of Christ. It should be a point of unity, not division.

# 7 - There is one God and Father of all.

There are references to the trinity in more than one place in Ephesians. In this section, we have seen the Holy Spirit, the Lord Jesus Christ and now we come to God the Father. By listing them separately Paul is emphasizing the unique roles of each member of the Triune God. The Jewish people in the Old Testament understood that **The Lord is our God, the Lord is one!** *(Deut. 6:4).* This was true then and true today. There is but one God. But in other passages in both Old and New Testament we see that the Father, Son and Holy Spirit are all called God, yet God is one. The mystery of the Trinity is just that, a mystery. We don't believe it because we can explain it, but because it is clearly revealed in the Scriptures.

> "Yet for us there is one God, the Father, from whom are all things and for whom we exist, and one Lord, Jesus Christ, through whom are all things and through whom we exist."
> (1 Corinthians 8:6)

*John MacArthur*
*"Our one God and Father, along with the Son and the Holy Spirit, is over all and through and in all. That comprehensive statement points to the glorious, divine, eternal unity that the Father gives believers by His Spirit and through the Son. We are God created, God loved, God saved, God Fathered, God controlled, God sustained, God filled, and God blessed. We are one people under one sovereign (overall) omnipotent (through all) and omnipresent (in all) God."*

---

# SECTION 2
## What happened when Jesus died?

### Ephesians 4:7-10

> "[7] But to each one of us grace was given according to the measure of Christ's gift. [8] Therefore it says,
> "When He ascended on high,
> He led captive a host of captives,
> And He gave gifts to men."
> [9] (Now this expression, "He ascended," what does it mean except that He also had descended into the lower parts of the earth? [10] He who descended is Himself also He who ascended far above all the heavens, so that He might fill all things.)"

## Christ the conquering hero.

The background for this fascinating passage is Psalm 68. The psalmist tells of a conquering hero returning from battle. He would have with him his formerly imprisoned captives that he has freed from enemy hands and now is bringing them home with him. He would be welcomed by cheering crowds who would give gifts to their returning hero. That is the image David uses in Psalm 68. Paul in Ephesians Four, under the inspiration of God, retells that story but adds one interesting change to the Old Testament image. The conquering hero in Ephesians Four is Jesus who has returned from the war against sin and death, and now the resurrected Jesus is returning to Heaven as a conquering hero and the liberated captives of the war are His children formerly in bondage but now are freed and part of His triumphant procession.

The one interesting difference in Jesus' triumphal procession is that in the Old Testament tradition, gifts were given to their conquering general, but now Jesus gives gifts to His people instead of receiving them. (Compare Psalm 68:17, 18 with Ephesians 4:8)

An old hymn that folks used to sing had this image in mind. It is sung from the perspective of those in Heaven welcoming Jesus home from battle as the conquering hero. Just imagine heavenly crowds joyfully welcoming him home.

> Look Ye Saints, the sight is glorious
> Look, ye saints! the sight is glorious:
> see the Man of Sorrows now;
> from the fight returned victorious,
> every knee to him shall bow;
> crown him, crown him,
> crown him, crown him,
> crowns become the Victor's brow.
>
> Hark, those bursts of acclamation!
> hark, those loud triumphant chords!
> Jesus takes the highest station;

*O what joy the sight affords!*
*crown him, crown him,*
*crown him, crown him,*
*King of kings and Lord of lords!*

The question comes, who are the captives that are being rescued and set free that this passage is talking about? That question is answered in verses nine and ten.

### Identifying the captives.

Verses 9 and 10 identify the one who has ascended high, the one who freed the captives as one who first descended to the lower parts of the earth. Let's see what that means.

Before Jesus died and rose again everyone who died, both good and evil, went to a place called Sheol. The Hebrew word "Sheol" is the place of the dead. It is traditionally described as a place in the lower parts of the earth. The Greek New Testament calls the place "Hades." We know from Luke 16 that Hades or Sheol had three parts to it. There was a place of torment for all the souls of the lost. There was a place of comfort for all the souls of believers who had passed on. Between the two places was a bottomless pit. When a person died, he was carried by the angels to Sheol. Today, when a lost person dies he goes to Sheol, sometimes called the grave, or Hell in the Bible. The body goes to the tomb and returns to dust but the soul and spirit, the non-material part of man, goes to Sheol.

But when Jesus died and rose again He freed the captives from the place of comfort and delivered them in triumphal procession to the Father. Today when believers die we go directly into God's presence (2 Corinthins 5:8). That was made possible because Christ removed sin which was the barrier keeping man from entering the actual presence of God. But for the unbeliever that barrier still remains so they must remain separated from God. In the last Judgment, the book of Revelation tells us what will happen to the lost who have been held in Hades all these years.

**"12 And I saw the dead, the great and the small, standing before the throne, and books were opened; and another book was opened, which is the book of life; and the dead were judged from the things which were written in the books, according to their deeds. 13 And the sea gave up the dead which were in it, and death and Hades gave up the dead which were in them; and they were judged, every one of them according to their deeds. 14 Then death and Hades were thrown into the lake of fire. This is the second death, the lake of fire. 15 And if anyone's name was not found written in the book of life, he was thrown into the lake of fire. "**
(Revelation 20:12-15)

With these images in mind here is what happened when Jesus died on the cross. His body was taken off the cross and put in a borrowed tomb (It was a borrowed tomb because He only needed it three days!) Jesus, Himself, soul and spirit, went to Sheol for three days. He didn't immediately ascend to the Father. After three days in Sheol He rose from the dead. His soul and spirit rejoined His body in the tomb, and He came out of the tomb. He told Mary not to cling to Him because He had not yet ascended to the Father. After 40 days being with His disciples and being seen by many, Jesus ascended to Heaven while the disciples watched. This was His triumphal procession as the conquering hero. All the believers who were in Sheol, in the place of comfort, also called Abraham's bosom, were freed and welcomed into Heaven with Jesus, their conquering Hero.

> **"Therefore it says,**
> **'When He ascended on high,**
> **He led captive a host of captives,**
> **And He gave gifts to men.'"** (Ephesians 4:8)

The earliest known statement of faith which dates back to the beginning of the New Testament era is called the Apostles Creed. It tells the same story:

## The Apostles Creed.

I believe in God, the Father Almighty,
  Creator of heaven and earth.
I believe in Jesus Christ, His only Son, our Lord,
  who was conceived by the Holy Spirit
  and born of the virgin Mary.
  He suffered under Pontius Pilate,
  was crucified, died, and was buried;
  He descended to hell.
  The third day He rose again from the dead.
  He ascended to heaven
  and is seated at the right hand of God the Father Almighty.
  From there He will come to judge the living and the dead.
I believe in the Holy Spirit,
  the holy catholic (universal) church,
  the communion of saints,
  the forgiveness of sins,
  the resurrection of the body,
  and the life everlasting. Amen.

The first section discussed seven great common beliefs that hold us in unity. They present a triune God, a God of unity. We also have one Lord Jesus, our Savior, who died on the cross and freed all the former prisoners of war, the believers who were in a place of waiting until sin could be paid for and He has taken all those believers into Glory. And so, this section is the final chapter of the redemption story, what happens to the believer when he dies. It is part of our foundational beliefs that give us hope and unify us.

This is what happened when Jesus died and rose again. The next question is what are the gifts mentioned that He gave to men? It may of course refer to rewards for the believers, but when you read on in Ephesians, the next section begins with gifts God has given to the church so both may be correct.

4:7-10

Let's now go to the next section which describes the gifts God has given to the church.

## SECTION 3
## The leadership and purpose of the church.

**Ephesians 4:11-16**

> "[11] And He gave some as apostles, and some as prophets, and some as evangelists, and some as pastors and teachers, [12] for the equipping of the saints for the work of service, to the building up of the body of Christ; [13] until we all attain to the unity of the faith, and of the knowledge of the Son of God, to a mature man, to the measure of the stature which belongs to the fullness of Christ. [14] As a result, we are no longer to be children, tossed here and there by waves and carried about by every wind of doctrine, by the trickery of men, by craftiness in deceitful scheming; [15] but speaking the truth in love, we are to grow up in all aspects into Him who is the head, even Christ, [16] from whom the whole body, being fitted and held together by what every joint supplies, according to the proper working of each individual part, causes the growth of the body for the building up of itself in love."

### Ephesians 4:11 and 12 - The Church leadership established by God.

Ephesians 4:11 and 12 is one of four passages in the New Testament that describe Spiritual Gifts. The others are 1 Corinthians 12-14, 1 Peter 4 and Romans 12. The uniqueness of Ephesians Four is that Ephesians specifically focuses on church leadership. The other passages are more general and apply to the entire church body. Every member of the body has been given spiritual gifts from God to use in building up one another. But Ephesians Four is unique. In the previous section, we read that when Christ ascended He "gave gifts to men." Ephesians 4:11 and 12 tells us what those gifts are. They are Apostles, Prophets, Evangelists and Pastors who can teach. These are specially gifted people that God has given to the church to develop it into a mature body of believers.

As Paul begins what will be three chapters on the church and how we are to live as victorious Christians in a broken world, he begins with the special leaders that God has given as gifts to the church. These special group of people are sent as foundation layers of the church and instructors and shepherds of the flock. Their purpose is to assist the body of Christ to grow into maturity and bring glory to God. Let's look at these four gifted leaders.

> **"And He (God) gave . . .**
> **Apostles**
> **Prophets**
> **Evangelists**
> **Pastor/Teachers"**

As with all spiritual gifts, they come from God, not man. The Holy Spirit distributes the gifts to each member of the body as He desires.  The purpose of the gifts is always to build the body, not the individual receiving the gifts (1 Cor. 12:7-11). God himself has chosen those who will fill these four roles in church leadership.

When we look at them in the order given it is like looking at God's game plan in church planting. They are given in the sequence needed to see a new church starterd and established and then nurtured to maturity.


**\*\*Leader Notes\*\***
There is one important matter we need to consider before we examine the four leadership gifts. If God has entrusted you with any of the leadership gifts, you need to see this as a divine trust, not an excuse to be a demanding or controlling person (2Cor 1:24, 1 Pet 5:3).  We have all seen leaders who were arrogant, abusers of

power or pastors who insist on obedience or submission to their positions. Leadership is a trust, and like salvation, it is of grace, not something we can boast in or use for personal power. It is grace and comes from God. We need a humble spirit without any desire for personal gain or importance. We serve God and should use our gift for the body, not for ourselves.

## 1. Apostles

> **"So then you are no longer strangers and aliens, but you are fellow citizens with the saints, and are of God's household, [20] having been built on the foundation of the apostles and prophets, Christ Jesus Himself being the corner stone."**
> (Ephesians 2:11, 12)

The Greek word we translate as apostle means one who is sent on a mission. His mission is to "Go boldly where no man has gone before." His calling is the uttermost parts of the earth.

When a house is built, the first thing to go in is the foundation and that can often define the house and determine how strong it will be. As we know, Jesus chose 12 who were to become the foundation of the church, with Christ Himself being the chief cornerstone. Judas was disqualified and replaced, and later Paul filled that role as the Apostle born out of season. The reference to the Apostles in Ephesians is a reminder that the church was built on special men. Today, the gift of church planting, foundation building and missionaries, are in a sense the gift of apostleship. These are the pioneers opening up new territory for the kingdom of God. They are starters, foundation layers. Pastors are the finishers. Sometimes one person does both roles but not always. Paul was a church planter and he appointed pastors to replace him when the foundational work was established and then he moved on.

> **"According to the grace of God which was given to me, like**

a wise master builder I laid a foundation, and another is building on it. But each man must be careful how he builds on it." (1 Corinthians 3:10)

"And thus I aspired to preach the gospel, not where Christ was already named, so that I would not build on another man's foundation;" (Romans 15:20)

## 2. Prophets

"It is he who will go as a forerunner before Him in the spirit and power of Elijah, to turn the hearts of the fathers back to the children, and the disobedient to the attitude of the righteous, so as to make ready a people prepared for the Lord." (Luke 1:17)

A prophet is one who speaks for God or proclaims the word of God. He normally did that in the context of the local church being planted. He was a strong authority, a man who called the people back to God. So, the first two categories in the first century were a team of church planters who went where the gospel had not been heard and established new churches. At that time, the apostle's ministry was sometimes accompanied by signs and wonders. By the end of the New Testament era the signs and wonders dropped off. Paul at the end of his ministry told Timothy to take a little wine to help his many stomach ailments, and he also left one of his trusted coworkers sick before returning to Jerusalem.

Today, the original offices of Apostles and Prophets are still echoed in our church planting teams who take the gospel to unreached people and proclaim with power the Word of God. God still changes lives by His great power.

One of the prophets in the time of Paul was Agabus. When Paul was about to leave for Jerusalem and would face imprisonment, Agabus was given words by the Holy Spirit to give to Paul.

> "[10] As we were staying there for some days, a prophet named Agabus came down from Judea. [11] And coming to us, he took Paul's belt and bound his own feet and hands, and said, "This is what the Holy Spirit says: 'In this way the Jews at Jerusalem will bind the man who owns this belt and deliver him into the hands of the Gentiles.'" (Acts 21:10,11)

Once a church is established then the offices of the evangelists and pastors build the church into a mature body of believers. It is about teamwork and unity. The community of God building the kingdom of God on the earth.

## 3. Evangelists

> "On the next day we left and came to Caesarea, and entering the house of Philip the evangelist, who was one of the seven, we stayed with him." (Acts 21:8)

Even though each of us as believers is a witness for Christ, one who shares the gospel with the unsaved, there is a special group of people with an empowered gospel message from God. Evangelists are a called group who present a clear understanding of the good news. If we were to describe the Apostles and Prophets as fishermen going out into the deep to find the fish, then the evangelist would be the one to draw in the nets and gather the catch into the boat.

> "[18] Now as Jesus was walking by the Sea of Galilee, He saw two brothers, Simon who was called Peter, and Andrew his brother, casting a net into the sea; for they were fishermen. [19] And He said to them, "Follow Me, and I will make you fishers of men." [20] Immediately they left their nets and followed Him." (Matthew 4:18-20)

## 4. Pastor/Teachers

> ". . . an overseer, then, must be above reproach, the husband of one wife, temperate, prudent, respectable, hospitable,

4:11-12

**able to teach, not addicted to wine or pugnacious, but gentle, peaceable, free from the love of money."**
(1 Timothy 3:1-7)

The evangelists bring people into the fold and the teaching shepherds feed, disciple and protect the flock from false teachers. Just as in the first century, God has called out and equipped special people and given them as a gift to the church. Today's pastors have a rich heritage and wonderful examples to follow in God's word. The Bible is also the best instruction manual.

The church of Ephesus was an amazing church that owed its maturity to the vast team of church planters and godly teachers that God sent them. They had Paul, Silas, Luke, Apollos, Aquilla and Priscilla, Epaphras, and others. When Paul left, he put his most trusted disciple in charge, Timothy. Later, the Apostle John became the main elder of the church in Ephesus. I guess we can call it God's church planting and building dream team.

Pastors, pray to the Lord of the harvest that He will send you special people to be part of your team. That is a prayer He loves to answer. As a pastor, be alert to recognize those people and work as a team, each member doing his role. A pastor was never meant to be a superstar doing everything

When godly leaders are fulfilling their assignment with joy then the people are free to exercise their gifts and become the kind of Christians God has called them to be.

## Ephesians 4:12-16 - Godly leaders build mature churches.

**"[12] for the equipping of the saints for the work of service, to the building up of the body of Christ; [13] until we all attain to the unity of the faith, and of the knowledge of the Son of God, to a mature man, to the measure of the stature which belongs to the fullness of Christ. [14] As a result, we are no**

**longer to be children, tossed here and there by waves and carried about by every wind of doctrine, by the trickery of men, by craftiness in deceitful scheming; [15] but speaking the truth in love, we are to grow up in all aspects into Him who is the head, even Christ, [16] from whom the whole body, being fitted and held together by what every joint supplies, according to the proper working of each individual part, causes the growth of the body for the building up of itself in love."**

Ephesians 4:12-16 is huge. If we only had this passage and nothing else to guide us as pastors and teachers, it would be a lifetime challenge just to see these lofty goals met. We could spend our entire lives praying and laboring to develop a church that lives up to these standards. The task can seem overwhelming. We also have an enemy who loves to point out our failures.

What can one person do? When that one person is a faithful believer, he or she is not alone, but is one person plus God. And that is what makes the impossible dream possible. With a dedicated leader, a godly team and Almighty God with us, we can see churches grow that honor Him and change our worlds. We can actually see a church like the one described in Ephesians 4:12-16.

### Here is a summary of what this passage teaches us about that church.

- It is equipped to take on God's assignments.
- It is active in the service of God, each member doing their part.
- The members are growing stronger in the Lord.
- There is a high degree of unity in the body; they have common purpose and goals.
- They are becoming more and more Christ-like.
- Because they are strong in faith and understanding of God's Word, they are not easily tricked by the enemy or led astray in

false teachings.

- They are known for being people of truth, have trusted reputations.

- There is a great sense of love in the church community and cooperation one with another.

- Because of their love for each other the lost world around them takes notice and some seek God.

Is that the church you want? At a pastors' conference a revival preacher told his audience the secret of revival in the church. He said, "Draw a circle on the ground and step inside of it and pray, "Lord, please revive everything inside this circle." A Godly church begins with a Godly pastor.

The final section of this chapter, as well as chapters Five and Six, describes the entire church, not just the leadership. It covers a multitude of topics involving relationships with family, each other and at work. It deals with moral life choices and personal disciplines that can define our lives. Finally, we see the veil lifted on the unseen evil world and the warfare we face each day. The good news is that God has provided ample protection for us as we do battle against the devil and his army.

## SECTION 4
## The life we are called to lead as Christians.
### (Ephesians 4:17-32)

Remember in Chapter Two Paul reminded the Ephesian believers that before they came to faith in Christ they were dead, deceived, depraved and doomed. Before their dark hearts and minds were brought into the light of God, they stumbled through life as slaves of their fallen natures. They were given over to all manner of sins. But God, rich in mercy, changed everything. Paul will now revisit that theme and amplify it. He will draw a contrast between the life

4:17-19

in Christ and the immoral life of the idolaters who reject the grace of God.

The Temple of Artemis was typical of Greek and Roman Temples dedicated to false gods. The pagan worshippers often had immoral practices as part of their religion. Paul, in this next passage, contrasts the life believers are to live compared to the temple worship and practices they had around them.

### Ephesians 4:17-19 – The beauty of truth and understanding contrasted with the error and darkness of the lost.

> "[17] So this I say, and affirm together with the Lord, that you walk no longer just as the Gentiles also walk, in the futility of their mind, [18] being darkened in their understanding, excluded from the life of God because of the ignorance that is in them, because of the hardness of their heart; [19] and they, having become callous, have given themselves over to sensuality for the practice of every kind of impurity with greediness." (Ephesians 4:17-19)

We have already been told in Ephesians 2:2-3 that we all walked:

> "[2]according to the prince of the power of the air, of the spirit that is now working in the sons of disobedience. [3] Among them we too all formerly lived in the lusts of our flesh, indulging the desires of the flesh and of the mind,"

Now we see that description expanded as Paul describes in detail the characteristics of a lost person in verses 17-20. (A parallel description is also found in Romans 1:18-32)

**Let's briefly look at each description given in these verses.**

### 1. Futility of their minds. (Ephesians 4:17)

> "Then the Lord saw that the wickedness of man was great

on the earth, and that every intent of the thoughts of his heart was only evil continually." (Gen 6:5)

The Fall of Man corrupted every part of man's being. Without God stepping in and changing our hearts and minds, our thoughts continually wander from God, and we pursue things that have no value for our souls. Without God, we live lives of emptiness and complete futility. Life becomes what Solomon described as chasing after the wind.

## 2. Darkened in their understanding. (Ephesians 4:18)

Have you ever been in a room when the lights are turned out or in a building when the power went out? It can be confusing. What do we do next when we can't see? Or, have you ever talked to a blind person? Did you realize that many of the words you used had no clear meaning to him? The blind have no understanding what colors mean. They don't know the difference between day and night. The lost person is described as a person in blindness, not having true understanding of God and the world. They think they know but it Is blinded knowledge. They are:

> "always learning and never able to come to the knowledge of the truth." (2 Timothy 3:7)

## 3. Excluded from the life of God. (Ephesians 4:18)

One day there will be a grand wedding feast called the Marriage Supper of the Lamb. God sent out invitations to everyone saying, "Whosoever will may come." But the invitation also says RSVP. (You need to respond to the invitation.) Until a person does that he will not be included on the guest list. Sadly, not everyone invited will attend the greatest celebration in history.

> "And he sent out his slaves to call those who had been invited to the wedding feast, and they were unwilling to come." (Matthew 22:3)

4:17-19

### 4. Filled with ignorance. (Ephesians 4:18)

A passage in Romans describes these very things in this list but shows that one condition leads to another and then to the next. It is a downward spiral.

> **"For even though they knew God, they did not honor Him as God or give thanks, but they became futile in their speculations, and their foolish heart was darkened. 22 Professing to be wise, they became fools."** (Romans 1:21-22)

Ignorance means lack of understanding, knowledge and awareness. Someone that is ignorant is described as being full of no understanding, full of nothing. When something is full there is no room for anything else. What a sad state to be in. Filled with nothing and no room for anything else.

### 5. Hardened hearts. (Ephesians 4:18)

The sinful heart is like concrete that turns from soft to hard. Once hardened it is very difficult to penetrate. That is why God has to give us new hearts of flesh to replace our hearts of stone, or concrete. Without God, the hardened human heart cannot make itself soft towards God; it is a hopeless condition. But remember those two very important words we saw in Chapter Two, "But God . . . "

### 6. They are callous. (Ephesians 4:19)

Hardened hearts are uncaring about the people around them. They don't see human suffering or the pain. They don't see because they don't care.  Do you know what the opposite is to callousness? The opposite is Jesus.

> **"When Jesus went ashore, He saw a large crowd, and He felt compassion for them because they were like sheep without a shepherd; and He began to teach them many things."** (Mark 6:34)

### 7. Given over to sensuality. (Ephesians 4:19)

The immoral practices of the city of Ephesus were legendary. Most particular were the activities associated with the Temple of Artemis. Paul was warning Christians that they were held to a higher standard. Today the moral decline in many societies is being fed by the mostly immoral entertainment industry and the availability of the INTERNET globally which, although it can be very helpful, it also has a very dark side as well. The message of the Word of God is just as valid for us today. God holds Christians to a higher standard than the pagan world.

### 8. Consumed with greed. (Ephesians 4:19)

It has been well said that love can wait but lust can't. It is all about whether we are focused on others or just on ourselves. Greed says, "I want money, my own pleasure, prestige and importance." The end of the spiral in this passage is a totally self-absorbed life, consumed with greed.

### Ephesians 4:20-24 – A call to God's higher standard.

> "... But you did not learn Christ in this way, [21] if indeed you have heard Him and have been taught in Him, just as truth is in Jesus, [22] that, in reference to your former manner of life, you lay aside the old self, which is being corrupted in accordance with the lusts of deceit, [23] and that you be renewed in the spirit of your mind, [24] and put on the new self, which in the likeness of God has been created in righteousness and holiness of the truth." (Ephesians 4:20-24)

Let me just paraphrase these four verses in my own words.

*We may have come from many of these sinful practices we see all around us. But God delivered us from this ugly life that had deceived us. When we were introduced to Jesus, we felt like we had just been given the most wonderful bath, cleansed through and through. Everything is new. Jesus changed our hearts and our behavior. Now we need to keep our eyes on Jesus and not the sin around us. We need to walk in the light as he is in the light and not be overtaken by the darkness again.*

## So, what is God's higher standard?

The next passage, verses 25-32, is the first set of instructions about Christian living that honors God and makes a life full. Are we going to have to give something up to have that kind of life? Yes, we will have to give up a life of futility, darkness, exclusion from God, ignorance, hardness of heart, callousness, unfulfilling sensuality and greed!

### Ephesians 4:25-32 – Practical instructions for Believers.

"[25] Therefore, laying aside falsehood, speak truth each one of you with his neighbor, for we are members of one another. [26] Be angry, and yet do not sin; do not let the sun go down on your anger, [27] and do not give the devil an opportunity. [28] He who steals must steal no longer; but rather he must labor, performing with his own hands what is good, so that he will have something to share with one who has need. [29] Let no unwholesome word proceed from your mouth, but only such a word as is good for edification according to the need of the moment, so that it will give grace to those who hear. [30] Do not grieve the Holy Spirit of God, by whom you were sealed for the day of redemption. [31] Let all bitterness and wrath and anger and clamor and slander be put away from you, along with all malice. [32] Be kind to one another, tender-hearted, forgiving each other, just as God in Christ also has forgiven you." (Ephesians 4:25-32)

Paul now finishes Chapter Four with a series of one and two-sentence instructions and reminders. Let's consider each of these brief but vitally important topics. Paul begins with honesty.

## Honesty

> "25 Therefore, laying aside falsehood, speak truth each one of you with his neighbor, for we are members of one another." (Ephesians 4:25)

The contrast of the church with the sinful practices of the Temple of Artemis are in view here. The immoral temple practices and false teachings had eroded all moral values in the society. The church in contrast is a godly community, a family put together by God and interdependent on each other. We need and love one another. The second great commandment is emphasized, "Love our neighbors as we love ourselves." We don't love when we are dishonest with each other. We should be acting like a loving family not a pagan society. Remember what Jesus said,

> "By this all men will know that you are My disciples, if you have love for one another." (John 13:35)

## Anger

> "26 Be angry, and yet do not sin; do not let the sun go down on your anger, 27 and do not give the devil an opportunity." (Ephesians 4:26-27)

Anger was a real problem in Ephesus, especially when their primary goddess was attacked. In Acts 19 we read of a riot that took place, and the crowds filled the large 25,000 seat public theatre and for two hours shouted allegiance to their false goddess. Paul's companions would not even let him go near the riot.

Paul reminds the believers that there is a place for anger, anger against sin, a righteous anger. Jesus demonstrated that type of anger and it is not sin. But anger without a righteous cause is just opening the door for Satan to get control of our emotions and lead us away from our devotion to Christ.

## Stealing vs. sharing

> "**28 He who steals must steal no longer; but rather he must labor, performing with his own hands what is good, so that he will have something to share with one who has need.**"
> (Ephesians 4:28)

There is a good example of this verse in the province of Cavite in the Philippines. A ministry called Working Hands takes street children who have trusted Christ at a Christian camp and provides a special place for them to stay. It is a place of compassion and hope. Healthy meals and spiritual guidance are provided to these young, formerly abandoned people. Not only are they loved and discipled in the ways of Christ, but vocational training is also provided for them. Hardened street kids, who spent their lives trying to survive by stealing food, soon find a loving family for the first time in their lives. They become cabinetmakers, welders, auto mechanics and the ladies learn to sew. They are helped in finding jobs when they graduate and connected to local churches. The former thieves now are able to help others like they have been helped. The motto verse for this agency should be no surprise, Ephesians 4:28.

## Careless and destructive speech

> "**29 Let no unwholesome word proceed from your mouth, but only such a word as is good for edification according to the need of the moment, so that it will give grace to those who hear.**" (Ephesians 4:29)

One of the major themes in the book of Proverbs is concerning our speech. Both constructive and destructive speech is addressed.

Actually, there are over 90 proverbs that give instruction on taming the tongue. Paul reminds us that there is great value when we use our words to build each other up. Healing words, not hurting words bring grace to the church. Anyone who has been in church leadership knows how damaging gossip, slander and unnecessary criticism is to the church. The most important thing pastors and teachers can do in this area is be great examples to the flock of what edifying speech looks like.

> **"A man who lacks judgment derides his neighbor, but a man of understanding holds his tongue."** (Proverbs 11:12)

## The Holy Spirit

> **"³⁰ Do not grieve the Holy Spirit of God, by whom you were sealed for the day of redemption."**
> (Ephesians 4:30)

There are many ways we can sin against the Holy Spirit. The Holy Spirit can be lied to, grieved, quenched, blasphemed, insulted, profaned and resisted.

To grieve means to cause injury or to cause one to suffer pain. When we quench the Holy Spirit, we interrupt His work, but when we grieve the Holy Spirit we hurt Him personally. We are born again by the Spirit, sealed into the body of Christ by the Holy Spirit, taught and kept by the Holy Spirit. When we love someone the last thing we want to do is hurt them. The context of this verse is an indicator that Paul is referring to a believer's moral life. Our sin causes pain to the Holy Spirit. Sin often has consequences we don't realize at the time of the offense. There are people hurt we weren't aware of.

A person recently talked to my wife and myself about his previous offense against us that had caused us much pain. He had come to realize just how much he had hurt us. When we sin, we cause the Holy Spirit much pain.

## Root of bitterness

> **"³¹ Let all bitterness and wrath and anger and clamor and slander be put away from you, along with all malice."** (Ephesians 4:31)

If you look at each word given in this verse and you ask yourself, what is the opposite of each of these words, you would have to say "love." When we love another, when we consider others more important than ourselves then we will treat them well. We will agree to differ on our opinions and not get angry or bitter or speak against them. And if we truly love them we will do one more thing and that is found in the next verse.

## Kindness and forgiveness

> **"³² Be kind to one another, tender-hearted, forgiving each other, just as God in Christ also has forgiven you."** (Ephesians 4:32)

How many times have you heard someone say, "I can forgive them but I can never forget what they did to me?" Is that real forgiveness? The test or standard of true forgiveness is given in this verse. How did God in Christ forgive us? Completely and unconditionally. When God forgives He never brings it up again. He never holds it against us again. When Jesus died on the cross for our sins, He said it was finished and it is. Now, when we say we forgive someone, don't revisit it, it's over. As one pastor said, "God tosses our sins into the depths of the ocean and then says, 'No fishing!'"

## Summary of Chapter Four

Chapter Four has just concluded with a course I would call Christian Living 101. Before we move on to the next class, Christian Living 201, it is worth making one observation. Both chapters two and four placed a strong emphasis on the depth of the sin in the human heart and the magnitude of the grace of God. That grace is especially important when we deal with life's most important relationships. That is the next chapter.

Now, onto Christian Living 201 in Chapter Five.

# Ephesians Chapter Five

# BUILDING BLOCKS
# OF A SOLID CHURCH

## Overview

Chapter Five continues the theme of Chapter Four, living the victorious Christian life. In this chapter, we find five major building blocks we need to build the body of Christ into the mature man God wants. Remember pastor, it all starts with you. You cannot expect the church to do what you won't do. They look to you to feed and lead by example. As you model these things the church will follow.

> **"Be imitators of me, just as I also am of Christ."**
> (1 Corinthians 11:1)

# Outline

**Five suggested preaching/teaching outlines for Chapter Five.**

**Section 1** | Ephesians 5:1- 2
The fragrance of Christ.

**Section 2** | Ephesians 5:3-5
The destructive power of immorality.

**Section 3** | Ephesians 5:6-14
Protecting the flock against false teachers.

**Section 4** | Ephesians 5:15-21
Maintaining a strong personal testimony.

**Section 5** | Ephesians 5:22-33
The Pattern for a christian marriage.

# Commentary

## SECTION 1
### The fragrance of Christ.

**Ephesians 5:1- 2**

> "Therefore be imitators of God, as beloved children; [2] and walk in love, just as Christ also loved you and gave Himself up for us, an offering and a sacrifice to God as a fragrant aroma."

Most of us have had the experience of walking into a flower shop, a perfume store or a place filled with beautiful incense. The fragrance was stunning and satisfying. Beautiful fragrances can be calming, inspirational and joyful. Do you know what smells wonderful to God? Love. The greatest fragrance of all time was when Jesus went to the cross to die for the sins of the world. Our passage refers to this moment in Old Testament language. In the book of Leviticus God gave the nation of Israel five offerings that were to be done at the great altar in the courtyard of the Tabernacle and then later at the Temple. Three of them were voluntary offerings and were a way for His people to worship, praise and offer thanksgiving and even rededicate their lives to God.

The other two offerings dealt with sin, and they were not voluntary. Every Israelite had to offer sin and guilt offerings. When sin was taken care of, then they could worship with the whole burnt offering or the peace offering or meal offering.

When Jesus died for us, He was, of course, the fulfillment of all five offerings. He paid for our sin nature and sin practices. He also did it all voluntarily and His sacrifice and submissive offering to God was acceptable, pleasing in the Father's sight. It was all a sacrifice of love as He *"gave Himself up for us, an offering and a sacrifice to God as a fragrant aroma."*

And now we as believers are called to love one another, and when we do, we become imitators of God because God is love. We are never more Christ-like than when we love each other

> "³⁴ A new commandment I give to you, that you love one another, even as I have loved you, that you also love one another. ³⁵ By this all men will know that you are My disciples, if you have love for one another." (John 13:34-35)

# SECTION 2
## The destructive power of immorality.

### Ephesians 5:3-5

> "³ But immorality or any impurity or greed must not even be named among you, as is proper among saints; ⁴ and there must be no filthiness and silly talk, or coarse jesting, which are not fitting, but rather giving of thanks. ⁵ For this you know with certainty, that no immoral or impure person or covetous man, who is an idolater, has an inheritance in the kingdom of Christ and God."

Recently I had a serious operation to remove a kidney. Our kidneys are about the size of a human hand and weigh less than one pound. The tumor that was growing there was not all that large but it was cancer and would kill me if I let it go. It was such a small thing and to remove it was painful, but the life of my entire body was at risk so it was worth the pain.

This passage is about a different type of cancer, one that destroys the body of Christ. Immorality was a way of life for the residents of ancient Ephesus. Temple prostitutes were considered a way of worship for the goddess Artemis. When an immoral person came to faith in Christ, they were like a cancer to the church unless they abandoned their former way of life. We are the bride of Christ, and our affections must be His and His alone.

But it wasn't just the obvious outward sexual sins that are warned against. There are also the jokes and unclean conversations that the Bible calls "coarse jesting" that not only defile the individual but cause others to stumble. For the one who is Christ's, we know our conversation should be different from the world. We should focus on those things which build up, not tear down. In today's society, we have our own pagan temples; they just look different. Much modern TV entertainment and movies have compromising activities and language. The INTERNET also has its dark side as we know.

> **"And now, dear brothers and sisters, one final thing. Fix your thoughts on what is true, and honorable, and right, and pure, and lovely, and admirable. Think about things that are excellent and worthy of praise. ⁹ Keep putting into practice all you learned and received from me — everything you heard from me and saw me doing. Then the God of peace will be with you."**
> (New Living Translation, Philippians 4:8-9)

Paul warns in Ephesians 5:3 that immoral practices must never be mentioned as part of the fellowship. He knew that even a small amount could ultimately consume and destroy the body. The reputation of God is at stake to an unbelieving world. This is particularly important with leaders. When a pastor falls in immorality the effect on the entire church is huge. It often opens the gates for more sin to come in. With the temptations, today it is critical for leaders to keep their eyes on Jesus. I was in a large meeting of pastors once when a pastor who was leading the meeting told an inappropriate joke. It was a very quiet, uncomfortable moment. We were all shocked, and no one knew what to do because it was so out of place. What he thought was some kind of cute story was in fact totally out of place from the mood of the meeting. As the day continued on there was a sense in all of us that we felt dirty or defiled. I have never had respect for that pastor since. We don't invite him anymore to lead meetings. Just one careless moment can actually damage a ministry.

> **"Set a guard, O Lord, over my mouth; Keep watch over the door of my lips."** (Psalm 141:3)

The story is told that when Alexander the Great was building his powerful army and conquering the world that word reached him that one of his soldiers, who was also called Alexander, was a drunkard. The soldier was also very careless with his life and was an immoral man. Alexander the Great called him into his tent and asked if these charges were true. The soldier admitted they were. The great general told the man, "You either change your ways or change your name!"

It is likely that everyone reading this book has known of a pastor who failed in his moral life and lost his family and ministry. The consequences of this sin are devastating. That is why the Bible has dozens of warnings about it.

The Roman Catholic Church has paid a painful penalty for sexual abuse within its ranks. In the past 60 years since the exposures of the abuses began, 25,000 priests have left the priesthood in the USA and 120,000 worldwide have left. Of course, the Catholic Church is not the only religious group to have immorality in its ranks. Numerous well-known TV preachers and pastors of protestant churches in many countries have fallen in shame. The point of all this is to say that decisions and life choices have consequences.

God has called us to sexual purity as the church.  Leaders often determine the moral atmosphere of the church.

> "3 But immorality or any impurity or greed <u>must not even be named among you</u>, as is proper among saints" (Emphasis mine)

We carry the name of God with us every day.  We must never drag His name into the dirt.

---

# SECTION 3

## Protecting the flock against false teachers.

### Ephesians 5:6-14

> "6 Let no one deceive you with empty words, for because of these things the wrath of God comes upon the sons of disobedience. 7 Therefore do not be partakers with them; 8 for you were formerly darkness, but now you are Light in the Lord; walk as children of Light 9 (for the fruit of the Light consists in all goodness and righteousness and truth), 10 trying to learn what is pleasing to the Lord. 11 Do not participate in the unfruitful deeds of darkness, but instead even expose them; 12 for it is disgraceful even to speak of the things which are done by them in secret. 13 But all things become visible when they are exposed by the light, for everything that becomes visible is light. 14 For this reason it says,
>
> > 'Awake, sleeper,
> > And arise from the dead,
> > And Christ will shine on you.'"

Every culture has idioms, phrases that have a second meaning. They can be quite interesting and often profound. One tribe in Central Africa has an idiom they use in describing a person who has been humbled or embarrassed by something. They call him "a very small person that has been cut in half. "In the Philippines, a man who has a mistress is described as "paddling his boat up two rivers." In the USA, there is today an accepted idiom we use when warning a person to not be deceived. The idiom is "Don't drink the Kool-Aid."

The origin of that idiom is quite interesting. Maybe you already know the story. In 1978 over 900 people died in the central American village called Jonestown in the country of Guyana. They had all moved there from America following their religious cult leader, Jim Jones, the pastor of Peoples' Temple. The move to Guyana was to set up a perfect socialist utopia, but it disintegrated and came under investigation. In the end, Jim Jones led the entire commune to drink cyanide laced Kool-Aid drink and commit mass suicide. Today whenever a person is thought to be believing something false or harmful it is said of him, "He drank the Kool-Aid."

In Ephesians Five Paul is in essence warning the church against drinking the Kool-Aid of the Ephesian society with its false religion and its intellectual and philosophical arguments. It may look like something delicious and satisfying, but it is poison for the soul. The believers had been delivered from darkness to light and now they needed to walk in the light of truth, not return to the darkness of deception.

In verse 14 Paul tells those who have compromised with the world that they need to return to Christ, awaken from their sleep and return to living the resurrected life in Christ. We are His and need to be alive with Him, not walking around among the corpses and tombs of a spiritually dead world.

## SECTION 4
### Maintaining a strong personal testimony.

## Ephesians 5:15-21

> "<sup>15</sup> Therefore be careful how you walk, not as unwise men but as wise, <sup>16</sup> making the most of your time, because the days are evil. <sup>17</sup> So then do not be foolish, but understand what the will of the Lord is. <sup>18</sup> And do not get drunk with wine, for that is dissipation, but be filled with the Spirit, <sup>19</sup> speaking to one another in psalms and hymns and spiritual songs, singing and making melody with your heart to the Lord; <sup>20</sup> always giving thanks for all things in the name of our Lord Jesus Christ to God, even the Father; <sup>21</sup> and be subject to one another in the fear of Christ."

After warning the believers about the dangers of flirting with the world, Paul continues his description of the victorious Christian life.

## 1. Avoiding minefields. (Ephesians 5:15-16)

> "<sup>15</sup> Therefore be careful how you walk, not as unwise men but as wise, <sup>16</sup> making the most of your time, because the days are evil."

If you were in a war zone and you had to walk across an open field but learned that an enemy had buried dangerous landmines all over the field, how would you walk? We live in a world where Satan, our enemy, is the prince and power. He hates us and has laid down every kind of trap and snare. It is like a minefield of evil and temptation. That is the type of image this passage describes. Our challenge is to be very vigilant, alert at all times. The good news is that God is aware of every pitfall, every danger zone, and the best use of our time in that danger zone is to listen to the only One who can safely get us through. The Bible is His road map through the minefield.

Another similar image given in Scripture is that you are walking in a forest and you know a very dangerous lion is loose. It is a lion that has had a taste of human blood and is looking for its next meal. How will you walk through that forest?

> **"Be sober [well balanced and self-disciplined], be alert and cautious at all times. That enemy of yours, the devil, prowls around like a roaring lion [fiercely hungry], seeking someone to devour."** (The Amplified Bible, 1 Peter 5:8)

**\*\*Leader Notes\*\***

This is a good time to have your class or congregation discuss ways to protect themselves from the enemy. What does it look like to be well-balanced and self-disciplined, alert and cautious?

## 2. Be intoxicated with God. (Ephesians 5:17-18)

> **"17 So then do not be foolish, but understand what the will of the Lord is. 18 And do not get drunk with wine, for that is dissipation, but be filled with the Spirit,"**

At some time, we have probably seen someone who was drunk. Some become violent, and others act just plain foolish. But the main symptom is the same for all, they are different from their normal behavior. They are no longer under their own control but under another control, the alcohol. The point of this passage is not primarily about drinking alcohol, but it is saying that in the same way a person chooses to place himself under the influence of alcohol and becoming drunk, a Christian should place himself under the total influence of the Holy Spirit.

I have read that the Greek word used in this passage for "drunk" is a word in the ancient world that was used to describe the tanning of leather. The hides were soaked until totally saturated in the brine, they were "drunk" in the brine solution. Likewise, we should be so filled with the Holy Spirit that we are drunk with Him, saturated, under His control.

Concerning the topic of the social drinking of alcohol. There are different views on this in the Christian circles, and you will need to come to your own conviction on the topic. But there is one thing this passage does condemn, along with every other passage in Scripture on the subject and that is becoming drunk with wine. It is foolishness. It is sin. There is one drunkenness, however, that is not only permitted, but actually commanded. In this passage we are commanded to be saturated with the Holy Spirit, intoxicated with God.

### 3. Building community relationships. (Ephesians 5:19-21)

> "**19 speaking to one another in psalms and hymns and spiritual songs, singing and making melody with your heart to the Lord; 20 always giving thanks for all things in the name of our Lord Jesus Christ to God, even the Father; 21 and be subject to one another in the fear of Christ.**"

What would our churches be like if we had a song in our hearts, the word of God in our conversations, appreciation and thankfulness in our attitudes? That is what this passage is describing. The answer to that question comes from the previous passage we looked at. When you have a community of believers who are filled (or drunk) with the Holy Spirit, then you have a fellowship intoxicated with love and living that out with each other.

God's children, who are filled with Him, play well with others because they consider others before themselves. Paul described this in Philippians Chapter Two, and he gave the greatest illustration in all of history of what that kind of love looks like:

> "**2Then make me truly happy by agreeing wholeheartedly with each other, loving one another, and working together with one mind and purpose.**
> **3 Don't be selfish; don't try to impress others. Be humble,**

thinking of others as better than yourselves. [4] Don't look out only for your own interests, but take an interest in others, too.

[5] You must have the same attitude that Christ Jesus had.

[6] Though he was God,
    he did not think of equality with God
    as something to cling to.

[7] Instead, he gave up his divine privileges;
    he took the humble position of a slave
    and was born as a human being.

When he appeared in human form,

[8] he humbled himself in obedience to God
    and died a criminal's death on a cross."

(New Living Translation, Philippians 2:2-8)

Maybe some of you are thinking, I have never seen or been a part of a church like that, a church where people thought of others before themselves, a church where joy and love seemed to overflow and where encouragement was the conversation of the day instead of finding fault with others.

Remember this is not something we can achieve, only God can do it, and He will if we as a people surrender to Him, are filled with His Spirit and obey Him. Even if we have never seen a church like the one being described, that doesn't mean it can't happen with us.

**"And may the Lord make your love for one another and for all people grow and overflow, just as our love for you overflows."** (New Living Translation, 1 Thessalonians 3:12)

That verse has a wonderful word in it, the word "overflow." That is how it can happen. One person filled with the Spirit loves another as God intended, and the love of God begins its contagious effect. Our part is to be that one and let the overflow begin.

## A personal story.

May I share a personal story? Years ago, I got sick with Leukemia and I was given two months to live. I spent almost seven months in a hospital cancer ward in Seattle in the USA. My wife and I decided that since life was so wonderful, then dying must be even better since God saved it to the end.  So, we decided if I was going to die that I would die well. Here is what we did. We had fun stories for our doctors and nurses each day and even held contests and gave out prizes for the winners. Staff from all over the large hospital came and participated. It was a great time of joy, in spite of the physical pain of my treatments. I can't even begin to tell all the stories that happened, all the doctors and nurses that came into my room after dark to talk about Jesus. What the world thinks is a time of sorrow and sadness became a time of joy, light, testimony and changed lives. It became an overflow of joy.  It was contagious but it wasn't a disease. It was Jesus.

## SECTION 5
## The pattern for a christian marriage.

### Ephesians 5:22-33

"²² Wives, be subject to your own husbands, as to the Lord. ²³ For the husband is the head of the wife, as Christ also is the head of the church, He Himself being the Savior of the body. ²⁴ But as the church is subject to Christ, so also the wives ought to be to their husbands in everything. ²⁵ Husbands, love your wives, just as Christ also loved the church and gave Himself up for her, ²⁶ so that He might sanctify her, having cleansed her by the washing of water with the word, ²⁷ that He might present to Himself the church in all her glory, having no spot or wrinkle or any such thing; but that she would be holy and blameless. ²⁸ So husbands ought also to love their own wives as their own bodies. He who loves his own wife loves himself; ²⁹ for no one ever hated his own flesh, but nourishes and cherishes it, just as

> Christ also does the church, [30] because we are members of
> His body. [31] For this reason a man shall leave his father and
> mother and shall be joined to his wife, and the two shall
> become one flesh. [32] This mystery is great; but I am speak-
> ing with reference to Christ and the church. [33] Nevertheless,
> each individual among you also is to love his own wife even
> as himself, and the wife must see to it that she respects her
> husband."

God established marriage between a man and a woman from the
beginning. Ephesians 5:22-33 teaches us not only how that relationship works, but more importantly, that marriage is a picture of
Christ and the church. That is why the marriage relationship is so
important, and it explains why it is under siege by Satan.

## The war on marriage today.

Fewer are getting married today. More couples today move in
together without marriage. The decline in the moral fabric in many
nations has produced a new thinking that marriage is outdated and
no longer relevant. And even among those who marry there is an
increase in marriages that are open to outside relationships instead
of faithfulness to one spouse.

Also on the rise is a new definition of marriage. Today men with
men and women with women form what is being called marriage
under a new progressive morality. This is a rapidly growing movement in many countries. But it is not new, is it? Listen to what Paul
wrote nearly 2,000 years ago:

> "[25] They traded the truth about God for a lie. So they wor-
> shiped and served the things God created instead of the Cre-
> ator himself, who is worthy of eternal praise! Amen. [26] That
> is why God abandoned them to their shameful desires. Even
> the women turned against the natural way to have sex and
> instead indulged in sex with each other. [27] And the men,
> instead of having normal sexual relations with women,
> burned with lust for each other. Men did shameful things

> with other men, and as a result of this sin, they suffered within themselves the penalty they deserved.
>
> **²⁸ Since they thought it foolish to acknowledge God, he abandoned them to their foolish thinking and let them do things that should never be done."** (Romans 1:25-28)

Today, all statistics show that the new generation, known as the Millennials, is showing the greatest departure from traditional values and marriage. They also have departed from most Biblical values. Many liberal writers today want to see the end of marriage itself. The church will face this storm more and more in the days ahead.

Now back to our passage – What does God say about marriage?

One observation to keep in mind just before we look at the husband/wife relationship is that the larger topic is the family, not just the husband and the wife. We will look at the children in Ephesians 6:1-9. As a pastor or teacher, you may want to deal with the Christian family as one theme from Ephesians 5:22-6:9.

Let's look at the main teachings of this section:

> **1. The relationship of a husband to his wife and family, and the issue of submission of the wife.**
>
> **2. The mystery of marriage and how it portrays the mystery of the church. This section is all about life's most important relationships.**

## 1. The relationship between the husband and the wife and the issue of submission.

It seems like the number one issue to many people is the submission of the wife in this passage. In the last section, we learned about building strong Christian community. You will notice the final verse exhorts all of us to *"be subject to one another in the fear of Christ."* The next verse, verse 22, is the first example of this principle, wives are to show submission to their husbands. Paul will deal with husbands afterwards.

It is very important for all of us to make sure we get our game plan of life from God and not from the world around us. On the subject of wives and submission to their husbands the secular world often takes great offense at the topic. Women's liberation has become a large movement in the Western world. Pro-choice advocates are mostly the ones in control of media and news and form the narrative today. At the center of much of the movement is the issue of abortion rights. It is all about rights, the rights to use their bodies how they want. They demand the rights to make their own decisions about all of life's opportunities and decisions without anyone telling them what to do. When the subject of a wife submitting to a husband is discussed the conversation soon becomes very angry. The idea of a woman submitting to any man is considered by some as a form of slavery.

So, as we look at what God says it is important to keep in mind just that — it is what God says, not what our current culture says, that matters. The word of God applies to all cultures and peoples and times. It is timeless and is always true.

### To submit or not to submit, that is the question.

There are men, even pastors, who are very dominating and demand wives to obey their every order and cite this verse to prove it. But the word "submit" is not the same as the word "obey" used to describe the parent/child relationship in Chapter Six. A wife is not to be a servant, or slave, under a master or ruler of a kingdom. Neither is she to be viewed or used as a piece of property like some religions view women. As a child of God, she is an equal, a joint heir of Christ. In Christ, there is neither male nor female, all are equal under God. He alone is our ultimate Authority.

Rather than subjugate the wife and control her, the husband, according to Ephesians 5:25-33, has the responsibility as the head of the household to love his wife, to protect his wife, be the provider of the family and overall spiritual leader of the family. It is a loving relationship.

When you look at any corporation, organization or government operation you will find a group of people who have agreed to follow a certain structure in order for the group to function. But we also understand that just because a person is the manager does not mean that he or she is a more important person than a salesperson. They are all equal as people but have different roles and when each person fulfills his/her role or function then everything operates like it is designed. What kind of business would succeed if everyone just did what they wanted? It would be chaos.

God designed the human race. In Genesis, the first couple were given a test not to eat of the tree of the knowledge of good and evil. The woman was deceived, the man followed, and they both sinned against God. As a result, a great curse was placed on the woman, the man, the serpent and the earth and ultimately the entire created universe. Here is what God said to the man and woman specifically:

> "**16 Then he said to the woman,**
> **"I will sharpen the pain of your pregnancy,**
>     **and in pain you will give birth.**
> **And you will desire to control your husband,**
>     **but he will rule over you."**
> **17 And to the man he said,**
> **"Since you listened to your wife and ate from the tree**
>     **whose fruit I commanded you not to eat,**
> **the ground is cursed because of you.**
>     **All your life you will struggle to scratch a living from it.**
> **18 It will grow thorns and thistles for you,**
>     **though you will eat of its grains.**
> **19 By the sweat of your brow**

> **will you have food to eat**
> **until you return to the ground**
> **from which you were made.**
> **For you were made from dust,**
> **and to dust you will return."**
> (New Living Translation, Genesis 3:16-19)

When God created woman, she was formed from a rib from the man. Not from the foot or from the head. She was taken from the side, near the heart. She is not the head of man or the servant of man but a partner.

But after the Fall, part of the woman's curse, because she was deceived and listened to the tempter rather than God, was that in the marriage the husband became the head of the wife.

Again, we find an illustration in the operation of a company. Think of it like the manager of a company. He has responsibilities to lead and the woman also has responsibilities. Both are equal as people before God and remain equal, but just have different functions. When a wife submits to that assignment willingly and when a husband fulfills his role to love his wife properly, then the wife will respect her husband and find great fulfillment before God. They operate not as a dictatorship but as a team. A winning sports team is not made up of all the same positions. They may be all equally important and equal members of the team and celebrate equally when they win a championship, but that would never happen if there was not order in the team and different positions and a coach. Different roles but one team.

To summarize, a godly marriage is a loving union between a responsible husband who is the spiritual head over the family and a willingly submissive wife to the husband's headship. This type of union demonstrates Christ as the head of the church. The godly wife who accepts her role has a strong sense of security under the husband's protection and provision and both husband and wife come under the protection and provision of Christ, our ultimate head. It is not just a beautiful picture, it is a beautiful relationship.

## 2. Marriage by design is a picture of the Church and is a mystery.

Ephesians Five calls marriage a "mystery." In Chapter Three we talked about the three types of mysteries in the Bible. This is one that was not understood in times past but revealed in the New Testament time. Marriage is a picture of Christ and the church as explained in this passage. That understanding would not have been known before Christ's coming and sacrificial death on the cross. But now we understand it.

We learned earlier that both Jew and Gentile believers are now joined in a new union called the church. They have become one body, the body of Christ. Now we see that same principle applied to the marriage union. Two distinct people become one flesh. And in that union, we see the man as a picture of Christ as the head of the church.

### Lessons we learn about the Church from a godly marriage. (5:25-33)

(Ephesians 5:25-30) In God's view the church is the most important entity in the universe. It was for the church that God the Son left Heaven and became flesh to die on the cross, to bear all our sins, to suffer the unimaginable horror of becoming sin for us. The Holy One became the most despicable thing in the universe so we could be adopted into His forever family. That sacrifice shows us what love is. And husbands are commanded to love their wives in the same way, sacrificially. One can only imagine what kind of churches and families we would see in the world today if we did this. A godly church begins with godly marriages and godly relationships in the body of Christ.

**(Ephesians 5:31-33)** In earlier chapters we looked at the mystery of the church, namely, God has taken both Jew and Gentile and formed them into something new, the church. Those who were separate people have become one new person in Christ. Paul returns to that description in verses 31-33 in describing marriage. The unity of the church members one to another, the unity of the Jewish believers with Gentile believers, the unity of Christ and His people are all part of the mystery of the church. Only God can make this happen. Now that great mystery is explained by the marriage relationship. The husband and wife, formerly two separate people, have been formed into one new flesh. It is a beautiful work of God.

**\*\*Leader Notes\*\***
The best way to communicate these great truths about Christ and the church is to be a model of a strong, godly marriage. If your relationship is not honoring to God, then your preaching and teaching will be powerless. If a pastor is overbearing, harsh or demanding to his wife, then she will be fearful and lose respect for him (verse 33). This will also reflect on the entire fellowship. When pastors demand respect and obedience, the church lives in fear. When pastors love their wives and their people, there is growth in the body. Healthy, loving marriages are the best soil for churches to grow

# BONUS SECTION

It is clearly stated that marriage is a picture of Christ and the Church. Ephesians Chapter Five focuses primarily on the relationship of the husband and the wife. It pictures the relationship of

Christ and the Church. But the marriage customs in the first century present a much larger story. Before we close out this chapter, I want to recommend that if you teach Ephesians that you add this topic to the lessons. It will be a great blessing to your people and to yourself. The Jewish betrothal system, the marriage ceremony and what follows is not only beautiful, but it also by Divine design pictures the second coming of Christ and what follows. The relationship of man and wife as seen is Ephesians Five is important, but it is only one piece of a much larger teaching of the church as the bride and Christ, our Bridegroom. Here is just a brief outline of Jewish marriage in the time of Christ.

## Marriage in Biblical times.

1. Cross-cultural marriage. A blending of two cultures but one party of the new couple will move to the others home country and culture and that becomes the new home. (Jesus is preparing a place for us. He will come again to take us to his home).

2. Proposal, acceptance.

3. Time of engagement – strong commitment level, just like marriage. When Joseph thought Mary had been unfaithful he was going to divorce her. Engagement was viewed like marriage, a complete, binding commitment to each other.

4. The groom calls for his bride. When the time for the wedding had arrived, the groom would go to the bride's house and shout for her by name and take his bride. (Jesus is coming again with a shout to call for His bride).

5. The bride was to be prepared, oil in lamp, faithful in her heart and just as a bride prepares for her wedding. She was ready to meet her future husband. (This is living for Christ today as we saw in Ephesians Five).

6. Then comes the wedding ceremony followed by the wedding

feast with the guests. (When the church is complete, all gathered in, then a great wedding supper of the Lamb, a celebration of the wedding will take place).

7. Then both the groom and bride leave their homes and cleave to one another to start a new home.

8. The bride takes the husband's name, the marriage is consummated and they, the new couple, become one flesh.

9. They move to a new home, all things become new. (The new earth with Christ dwelling with us).

As you can see there is much more that can be studied and shared. The husband and wife relationship described in Ephesians is a part of the larger Biblical story. It is also prophetic pointing to the second coming of Christ.

# Summary of Chapter Five

Numerous important topics were handled in Chapter Five. The primary theme was walking with Christ in a way that honors Him and builds his body, the Church. It concluded with the keys to a successful marriage, and how a Godly marriage is a powerful testimony to the lost world. It pictures Christ and the Church.

Chapter Six will deal with two other relationships, children and parents and employers and employees. Both Chapters Five and Six lead to unity in the body, unity in the family, unity in the workplace. Unity.

Then we will also learn about the most important war in the world.

# Ephesians Chapter Six

# WAR
## OF THE WORLDS

## Overview

Whether we are still a child, a parent or an employee of a company we all have a role to play in God's community on earth, called the church. And each role is important for our testimony and our witness for our Savior. After Paul gives instructions for each of these different people, he then unveils the dark underground of demons and our enemy Satan who wants to destroy our testimony and defile the church. Paul then gives us clear instructions how we can resist and defeat our enemy

# Outline

**Section 1** | Ephesians 6:1-4
Instructions for families.
      for children. (Ephesians 6: 1-3)
      for fathers. (Ephesians 6: 4)

**Section 2** | Ephesians 6:5-9
Instructions for the workplace.
      for employees. (Ephesians 6:5-8)
      for employers. (Ephesians 6:9)

**Section 3** | Ephesians 6:10-20
The invisible war
      The war to end all wars. (Ephesians 6:10-12)
      The armor of God. (Ephesians 6:13-20)

**Closing Remarks** | Ephesians 6:21-24

You may want to combine the first two outline topics into one message about the responsibilities of each of us in the community of God to be obedient to our calling. Whether we are children, fathers, parents, employees or employers, each of us has a vital role to play in the body of Christ.

# Commentary

---

## SECTION 1
## Instructions for families. (Ephesians 6:1-4)

### Instructions for children. (Ephesians 6:1-3)

> "Children, obey your parents in the Lord, for this is right. [2] Honor your father and mother (which is the first commandment with a promise), [3] so that it may be well with you, and that you may live long on the earth."

There is no doubt that the evil environment of the pagan city of Ephesus provided many temptations and distractions for families, especially the children. Paul reminds families to instruct their children in God's ways. He quotes the fourth commandment and reminds children that a promise of God's blessing on their lives comes with obeying this commandment. The future message of the gospel is entrusted to families and to their children. When families raise godly children, they are providing for a godly future for everyone. Early on, a child needs to understand that they are salt and light for the society where they live.

> "13 You are the salt of the earth; but if the salt has become tasteless, how can it be made salty again? It is no longer good for anything, except to be thrown out and trampled under foot by men.
> 14 You are the light of the world. A city set on a hill cannot be hidden; 15 nor does anyone light a lamp and put it under a basket, but on the lampstand, and it gives light to all who are in the house. 16 Let your light shine before men in such a way that they may see your good works, and glorify your Father who is in heaven." (Matthew 5:13-16)

The overall task of raising Christian children is best pictured in the life of Jesus when He was young.

> "And Jesus kept increasing in wisdom and stature, and in favor with God and men." (Luke 2:52)

This verse in Luke shows that a parent needs to make sure their children grow in the following four ways:

### 1. Emotionally, intellectually. ("wisdom")

A loving, nurturing home is the foundation for raising children who are safe, secure and grow up ready to deal with a world in chaos. Good parents also pay attention to the things children learn. Both emotional development and educational growth need to be determined or carefully overseen by parents. Children are like blank canvases when they are born. They become works of art when parents, like artists, fill the canvas with colors and ideas and wonder. But education and cultivating wonder are not enough. When the word of God is central to the training of children they learn God's perspective on life. Wisdom will then be passed on and nurtured.

### 2. Physically. ("stature")

Physical growth and health are also a responsibility of loving parents. It matters what a child eats. Many illnesses and obesity problems are direct consequences of poor life habits and nutrition, even lack of exercise. If children today spend their days eating unhealthy foods and watching TV or playing video games all day, then their bodies and minds will suffer greatly. Parents are responsible to help develop the total person, and that includes taking care of the physical body.

### 3. Spiritually. ("favor with God")

Spiritual growth will be determined by several factors. The most important is when a child is raised in a home where the parents are committed Christians who love each other and God's word is honored. Children need *to see* the Christian life, not just hear about it at church. Another factor is the friends they have. Most importantly, being led to a saving faith in Jesus Christ at an early age is critical. Spiritual growth in our children is a lifelong commitment for parents.

### 4. Socially. ("favor with man")

We all know people that just can't get along with others.  The Bible exhorts us to be at peace with all men whenever possible (Romans 12:18). Parents play the most important role in modeling and helping their children to develop good social skills. When parents care about others, your children see that. Since we are born in sin, a child left to his own way will grow up selfish and even anti-social. If he or she is to play well with others and share, then these traits have to be taught.

When children grow up in homes that emphasize these life skills, they will learn early to honor and love their parents and the promise of God is that it will go well with them.

### Instructions for fathers. (Ephesians 6:4)

> **"Fathers, do not provoke your children to anger, but bring them up in the discipline and instruction of the Lord."**

One of the great tragedies in modern society is the growing number of single parent families. Most frequently, the man is the one who leaves. Godly fathers who are faithful to their wives and to their children are becoming a vanishing species.

In the Bible both parents are responsible before God to raise their children to fear and love God. They need to be in agreement and work together. But this verse singles out the fathers. Why? In Chapter Five we looked at marriage and how it is the picture of the church with Christ as the head. The man is the spiritual head of the wife and that includes being the spiritual head of the family. Many men leave the spiritual training of the children to the mothers, but ultimately that is not the best pattern God has designed for the family. A godly man needs to step up to his God-assigned responsibility of family headship, and when he does he will have the respect of his wife and his children.

Verse Four reveals two things that are very important for fathers to pursue. One command is a negative and the other is a positive. On the negative side, fathers are to avoid domineering or demanding attitudes or an approach to their children which drives them to anger. Paul must have seen in Grecian and Roman society a trait in the men which drove children away instead of drawing them closer to the family. A father can be a godly example and leader in his family without being a dictator.

The positive command to the father is to take the lead in providing both consistent and loving discipline as well as Christian instruction for the children. A father who does these things will be respected by his children. His wife should also be a supportive partner in both of these commands.

## SECTION 2
### Instructions for the workplace. (Ephesians 6:5-9)

# Instructions for workers, employees.

## Ephesians 6:5-8

> "⁵ Slaves, be obedient to those who are your masters according to the flesh, with fear and trembling, in the sincerity of your heart, as to Christ; ⁶ not by way of eye service, as men-pleasers, but as slaves of Christ, doing the will of God from the heart. ⁷ With good will render service, as to the Lord, and not to men, ⁸ knowing that whatever good thing each one does, this he will receive back from the Lord, whether slave or free."

The biblical era had a system of landowners and field workers. People who lost their financial security often had to enter into a form of debt bondage. They willingly served a master in order to pay off the debt they owed. Even though there were other types of slavery in the Old Testament world, the debt-bondage system was quite widespread. When a certain period of time had elapsed or the debt was paid off, the slave was set free by the master.  If a slave wanted to stay with that master, he could choose to become a lifetime slave or servant under that master. He became a willing bond servant.

The New Testament has 24 references to bond servants. Paul frequently referred to himself as a bond servant of Christ. In the book of Philippians Paul not only referred to both Timothy and himself as bond servants, but also tells us that Jesus Christ himself became a bond servant of God by His own choice.

> "Paul and Timothy, bond-servants of Christ Jesus, to all the saints in Christ Jesus who are in Philippi, including the overseers and deacons:"(Philippians 1:1)

> "⁵ Have this attitude in yourselves which was also in Christ Jesus, ⁶ who, although He existed in the form of God, did not regard equality with God a thing to be grasped, ⁷ but emp-

**tied Himself, taking the form of a bond-servant, and being made in the likeness of men."** (Philippians 2: 5-7)

In our modern times the closest thing we have to that system is the relationship between employers and employees. The principles of the master/slave relationship in the New Testament are helpful guidance for us today in the workplace.

If you are an employee of some person or company, you should have one goal. That goal is to work faithfully as if your boss were Jesus Himself. You should not be there to make yourself important but to make Jesus proud of you. You should work in such a way that others speak well of Jesus. Your purpose in the company is, with sincere heart, to make the company successful. If you do these things, you honor God, and one day God will honor your service. Just do it all for Jesus.

## Instructions for employers, bosses.

### Ephesians 6:9

> **"And masters, do the same things to them, and give up threatening, knowing that both their Master and yours is in heaven, and there is no partiality with Him."**

If you are a company executive, a boss, a manager or anyone who has authority over company workers the same rules apply. Everything you do should be to honor God. He is your ultimate Boss. You serve a loving Father in Heaven and you should reflect godly attitudes and attributes in your leadership. This is not to be a domineering role but a leading role. Good leaders don't have to threaten their workers or have them living in fear but they treat workers respectfully while providing clear and decisive direction. Good workers love to work for good employers and everyone benefits. A workplace like this speaks well for the church.

# SECTION 3
## The invisible war (Ephesians 6:10-20)

### The war to end all wars. (Ephesians 6:10-12)

> "[10] Finally, be strong in the Lord and in the strength of His might. [11] Put on the full armor of God, so that you will be able to stand firm against the schemes of the devil. [12] For our struggle is not against flesh and blood, but against the rulers, against the powers, against the world forces of this darkness, against the spiritual forces of wickedness in the heavenly places."

When you see the word "finally," what do you think? Maybe you think it means, "We are almost finished, just one more point and then it is over." But the tense of the Greek word actually means "The moment you have been waiting for has arrived. I have saved a very important teaching to finish the letter." Paul is saying, "As I come to the end of my letter, I don't want you to miss this. Pay attention!"

In Ancient Greece, a popular sport was wrestling. This section on Spiritual warfare uses that picture. Just as wrestling is a strenuous struggle between two people, there is another struggle being portrayed. This struggle is not against a physical opponent but a spiritual one, against the powers of darkness all around us. It is not only unseen and intense, but it requires a different type of strategy, an invisible war with eternal consequences. The good news is that God has given us much information about our enemy and He has provided a special protection for us along with His strategy for victory.

### The dark side.
One of the most significant movies of our times has been the Star

Wars series. It was built around an invisible force which man could access. It had a good side, and of course there was "the dark side of the force." In the Bible, we learn that there is an invisible world around us, a spiritual world. Unlike Star Wars, it is not an impersonal force like gravity, but it is very personal. God, Satan, angels and demons are very personal and real even though we can't see them with our physical eyes. There is great and wondrous beauty in God's universe, but on the other side there is the dark side. Paul helps lift the veil of mystery about that spiritual darkness in this passage and describes a great war between God's angelic army and the demonic world. He also reveals how we can be victorious against our very powerful enemy.

There are two main topics we need to understand as believers in Paul's final instruction to the church in Ephesians. The first is about the realm of the spiritual war we are in. What is going on behind the scenes?

The second is about the spiritual armor, or protection God has given us for our protection in this great war. It is a war between two worlds, God's world and Satan's world. We begin first with understanding the nature of the war and learn about our enemy.

## A brief history of the dark world.

In eternity past only God existed, Father, Son and Holy Spirit. But for reasons He alone fully knows, God created the heavens and the earth, and everything contained therein. God created angels. Our knowledge of them is somewhat limited but the Scripture gives us glimpses into the wondrous world of celestial beings. Words like servants, guardians, warriors, cherubim, seraphim and others stir our imagination. The highest rank of these spirit beings is called Cherubim. They are associated with the throne of God and worship. It was a Cherub that guarded the way to the tree of life after the fall of man. God later would instruct Moses to have two Cherubim placed on the Mercy Seat, the cover of the Ark of the Covenant. Their wings covered and protected the place where the blood of the sacrifice was placed on the Day of Atonement.

Of all the Cherubim there was one that became consumed with his beauty. He used the free will God had given him to make a grave choice, to reject God as God. His name was Lucifer or the "Shining One." Isaiah gives us a glimpse of his attitude and fateful decision.

> "12How you have fallen from heaven,
> O star of the morning, son of the dawn!
> You have been cut down to the earth,
> You who have weakened the nations!
> 13 "But you said in your heart,
> 'I will ascend to heaven;
> I will raise my throne above the stars of God,
> And I will sit on the mount of assembly
> In the recesses of the north.
> 14 'I will ascend above the heights of the clouds;
> I will make myself like the Most High.'" (Isaiah 14:12-14)

What Lucifer was saying to God was "You are sitting in my seat, I want it." He led a rebellion that resulted in a great number of the angels foolishly changing sides and following him as their lord.

> "3 Then another sign appeared in heaven: and behold, a great red dragon having seven heads and ten horns, and on his heads were seven diadems. 4 And his tail swept away a third of the stars of heaven and threw them to the earth." (Revelation 12:3-4)

> "7 And there was war in heaven, Michael and his angels waging war with the dragon. The dragon and his angels waged war, 8 and they were not strong enough, and there was no longer a place found for them in heaven. 9 And the great dragon was thrown down, the serpent of old who is called

the devil and Satan, who deceives the whole world; he was thrown down to the earth, and his angels were thrown down with him. [10] Then I heard a loud voice in heaven, saying,

> 'Now the salvation, and the power, and the kingdom of our God and the authority of His Christ have come, for the accuser of our brethren has been thrown down, he who accuses them before our God day and night.'"

(Revelation 12:7-10)

The Bible lists over 50 names, titles and descriptions for Lucifer after that. The most common names given to this fallen Cherub are the Devil and Satan, which describe him as a destroyer, accuser and deceiver, the prince of lies and darkness. He is the self-proclaimed enemy of God and all of God's children. The most significant passage is an amazing description given to Ezekiel by God in Chapter 28. After God gives a message of judgment of the prince of the city of Tyre for its wickedness, God then focuses on the real power behind the throne and addresses the one he calls the King of Tyre who is Satan.

> "[11] Again the word of the Lord came to me saying, [12] "Son of man, take up a lamentation over the king of Tyre and say to him, 'Thus says the Lord God,
> "You had the seal of perfection,
> Full of wisdom and perfect in beauty.
> [13] "You were in Eden, the garden of God;
> Every precious stone was your covering:
> The ruby, the topaz and the diamond;
> The beryl, the onyx and the jasper;
> The lapis lazuli, the turquoise and the emerald;
> And the gold, the workmanship of your settings and sockets,
> Was in you.
> On the day that you were created
> They were prepared.
> [14] "You were the anointed cherub who covers,

And I placed you there.
You were on the holy mountain of God;
You walked in the midst of the stones of fire.
<sup>15</sup> "You were blameless in your ways
From the day you were created
Until unrighteousness (evil) was found in you.
<sup>16</sup> "By the abundance of your trade
You were internally filled with violence,
And you sinned;
Therefore I have cast you as profane
From the mountain of God.
And I have destroyed you, O covering cherub,
From the midst of the stones of fire.
<sup>17</sup> "Your heart was lifted up because of your beauty;
You corrupted your wisdom by reason of your splendor.
I cast you to the ground;" (Ezekiel 28:11-17)

Some ask, "Did God create the Devil?" The answer is God created a beautiful, shining being called Lucifer, a glorious creation who by his own free choice made himself the Devil. As a fallen angel, sin consumed him, and he now leads an army of heavenly deserters obsessed with hurting God and damaging all His creation. That is the very brief history. Now the really bad news. He hates you. You are on his radar screen as an enemy invader into his world where he is the prince and power. But there is also some good news.

> "You are from God, little children, and have overcome them; because greater is He who is in you than he who is in the world." (1 John 4:4)

Because we have been purchased by the blood of Jesus Christ we are His possession, not Satan's. We have the Holy Spirit to guide and protect us, not the unholy spirit. We are equipped to be more than conquerors. And in Ephesians Six Paul gives us hope when he describes the armor of God which will keep us strong in the great war we face each day with our enemy — a spiritual war. It is war described in Ephesians Six as being waged by a powerful dark leader that has a battlefield of demonic soldiers who follow his evil command. Our battle is against:

> **"the rulers, against the powers, against the world forces of this darkness, against the spiritual forces of wickedness in the heavenly places."** (Ephesians 6:12)

### "rulers." *(arche)*

Arche means "beginning" or "first." In this context, it means those who are first in power and authority. They are the origin, the active cause of the spiritual darkness of the world.

### "powers." *(exousia)*

Refers to beings " in authority or power." Those with jurisdiction over others.

### "world forces of this darkness." *(kosmokrator)*

Comes from two Greek words — kosmos (world) and krateo (to hold). This word is only used once in the Bible and refers to Satan as the lord of this world, the prince of this age.

### "spiritual forces of wickedness in the heavenly places."

Three different Greek words make up the phrase and the meaning is one who is spiritual but the spiritual influence is one of depravity, wickedness, evil purposes and desires. And the third word tells us this takes place in the clouds or lower heavens. Satan is called the "prince and power of the air." The headquarters of evil are in the domain of the earth and its atmosphere. This is the capital city of the kingdom of darkness. Jesus said He would build His church literally at the gate of hell itself, the place where Satan reigns for this season.

This four-fold description of our enemy and his dark army emphasizes the reality, extent and influence he has. The good news is that this age is not going to reign in the age to come but for now we face a real foe and live on a real battlefield.

Even though they are a powerful and very organized army we have a greater General and more powerful army on our side. Our strength is in the Lord and the power of His might. He is not only on our side, He is with us every step. This is the war of the worlds, the war between light and darkness, good and evil. It is also the war that will be the end of all wars.

Now let's look at the special armor, or protection God has provided for us, His soldiers.

### The armor of God. (Ephesians 6:13-20)

"[13] Therefore, take up the full armor of God, so that you will be able to resist in the evil day, and having done everything, to stand firm. [14] Stand firm therefore, having girded your loins with truth, and having put on the breastplate of righteousness, [15] and having shod your feet with the preparation of the gospel of peace; [16] in addition to all, taking up the shield of faith with which you will be able to extinguish all the flaming arrows of the evil one. [17] And take the helmet of salvation, and the sword of the Spirit, which is the word of God. [18] With all prayer and petition pray at all times in the Spirit, and with this in view, be on the alert with all perseverance and petition for all the saints, [19] and pray on my behalf, that utterance may be given to me in the opening of my mouth, to make known with boldness the mystery of the gospel, [20] for which I am an ambassador in chains; that in proclaiming it I may speak boldly, as I ought to speak."

The Greek words Paul used when he commanded us to put on the entire armor of God were actually very strong language. Here is how one graduate of Greek studies paraphrases Ephesians 6:13:

*"I command you to put on yourself every piece of the armor*

*of God. Do this once and leave it on for eternity. Do this so you will be empowered by God and made able by Him to stand against the deceit, the tricks, and the methods the devil brings against you. You must take armor upon yourself in order to resist in evil times, and having done this to yourself you will be able to stand forever against the devil as you intentionally purposed to do."* Richard Keim

As you can see from this translation, the emphasis is very strong that this is something we need to do. It won't just happen by itself. If you have seat belts in a car and refuse to put them on, you will not be protected in an accident. Try to imagine that you are in the Roman army in the first century and your commanding general assembles you as an elite company of fighting men and tells you that tomorrow you will fight for Rome against the fiercest enemy you will ever encounter. The general then has new armor brought in that has been specifically designed just for you to wear to face that specific enemy. He lays all the pieces out and explains each piece and then commands you to put it on. It would be foolish to ignore that protection.

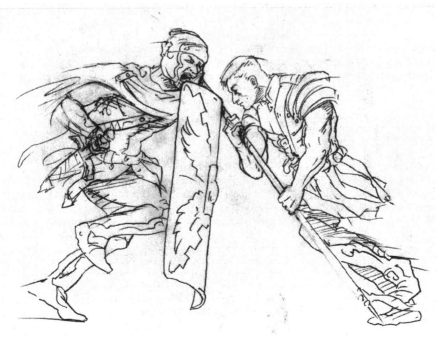

A Roman centurion
in his armor in the
time of Paul.

# The armor of God.

### The belt of truth. (Ephesians 6:14)

The belt in Roman armor was the foundational piece. It anchored the other pieces and held the weapons. And so it is with truth. If we don't have a firm foundation in God's truth, then nothing else matters. No soldier would fight for something he did not believe in. But when we know something is true, we will die for it.

> **"Jesus said to him, "I am the way, and the truth, and the life; no one comes to the Father but through Me."** (John 14:6)

When we know that Jesus is the Truth, then nothing can stop us. The truth is simply what is real. Jesus is real, Heaven is real, Hell is real, sin is real and salvation is real when our faith is placed in Jesus. We can be mocked, ridiculed, resisted and even killed, but when we are clinging to what is true, we win.

> **"[37] But in all these things we overwhelmingly conquer through Him who loved us. [38] For I am convinced that neither death, nor life, nor angels, nor principalities, nor things present, nor things to come, nor powers, [39] nor height, nor depth, nor any other created thing, will be able to separate us from the love of God, which is in Christ Jesus our Lord."** (Romans 8:37-39)

When we know the truth, we are set free. When we know the truth, we fear no man or demon. When we know Jesus, we know the truth. Our foundation is strong and secure. We know Satan is a liar from the beginning. He hates the truth we have in Christ.

## The breastplate of righteousness. (Ephesians 6:14)

The Roman breastplate protected the heart and vital organs. In the spiritual world, the heart and vital parts refer to the seat of the emotions. If a person is described as having a good heart, we think of that person as being kind or generous. A peaceful heart defines a person who is at rest with God and his neighbor.

Righteousness is a state of being right with God. When a person puts their faith in Christ, he is forgiven. He is declared as being in right standing with God. He is pardoned from having to pay for sins he is responsible for because Jesus paid it all on the cross in his place. All unrighteousness is removed from his record. There is no greater peace in life than knowing we are right with God. This is a prime target of our enemy. He accuses us that we are not worthy of being God's child. Satan wants to destroy our peace of heart.

### How do we put on righteousness?

Putting on the breastplate of righteousness means that we believe and thank God for what He has done in our lives. When we acknowledge to God that our salvation is based on the cross of Christ and our pardon from sin has been accomplished by the shed blood of our Savior, then we accept that His righteousness has been put on our account. His substitutionary death has replaced our unrighteousness with His righteousness. We are not perfect but He is and He is our defender against all enemy attacks. He is our breastplate, He is the protector of our hearts. He is our peace in the battle. Satan's lies cannot harm us.

Remember, the Roman breastplate was a very heavy piece with a front panel and a rear panel. It was placed on the soldier and covered his front and back. Our righteousness is put on us, we don't put it on ourselves. We are sinners saved by grace and the righteousness of Christ is placed on us by God, our commanding General.

> "He made Him who knew no sin to be sin on our behalf, so that we might become the righteousness of God in Him."
> (2 Corinthians 5:21)

## Feet fitted for readiness with the gospel of peace. (Ephesians 6:15)

> "How beautiful are the feet of them that preach the gospel of peace, and bring glad tidings of good things!"
> (Romans 10:15)

A soldier's shoes were vitally important because of the types of roads and terrain he walked over. Those shoes were part of a successful war campaign. In the illustration, the shoes are described as having an adequate preparation in the Gospel. Without a clear understanding and readiness in the Gospel, just like a soldier with poor footwear, we can stumble in the battle.

To preach the gospel we need to understand and be able to share the gospel. To have a faulty or false gospel is like having no shoes at all for our battle. There is no protection. We need to be students and defenders of the Word of God. It is the source of the good news, our message.

> "Now I make known to you, brethren, the gospel which I preached to you, which also you received, in which also you stand, [2] by which also you are saved, if you hold fast the word which I preached to you, unless you believed in vain. [3] For I delivered to you as of first importance what I also received, that Christ died for our sins according to the Scriptures, [4] and that He was buried, and that He was raised on the third day according to the Scriptures. . ."
> (1 Corinthians 15:1-4)

To be ready for battle we need a clear understanding of how a person comes to Christ. The better we understand God's word the more we will be effective as soldiers of the Lord.

## The shield of faith. (Ephesians 6:16)

As we learned earlier, Satan has around 50 titles and descriptions. Two of his most notorious are "accuser of the brethren" and the "deceiver." Attacks from him come constantly. They are like a steady barrage of burning arrows coming towards us. Roman soldiers defended against the arrows from the enemy by holding up their shields.  So, what is our shield in the spiritual war?  Faith. It is simple but powerful. We are saved by faith. We walk by faith, we live by faith and we fight by faith. And we will win by faith!

> **"And without faith it is impossible to please Him, for he who comes to God must believe that He is and that He is a rewarder of those who seek Him."**
> (Hebrews 11:6)

When Job was assaulted by Satan and robbed of his children and possessions, he responded by clinging to his faith in God by saying, ***"Though He slay me, yet will I trust Him"*** (Job 13:15).  When life was at its lowest and the attacks of the enemy were at the worst, Job only had one thing to hold him up, his faith. Nobody was on his side but God.

> - Satan says to you, "You are not a child of God."
> - Satan says you have sinned and are not worthy to be claimed by God.
> - Satan knows and reminds you of things done in the past.
> - Satan causes you to doubt that God cares about you. But even when it gets really hard and sometimes confusing, return to what you know and believe. I have prayed things like this:

> *"Whosoever shall call on the Name of the Lord will be saved. I trust Your promises.  I have been saved by grace through faith and no one, not even the Devil, can snatch me out of*

*Your hand, Lord. I am not perfect but I am forgiven. Thank you Lord for being my Savior and for being with me now in this hard moment.*

This passage says that faith can extinguish all, not just some, but all of the attacks, the flaming arrows of the enemy. Every single one of his lies, false claims and doubts — all of them.

## The helmet of salvation. (Ephesians 6:17)

The Roman soldier's helmet was firmly attached so it wouldn't come off in battle. What good is a helmet if you could lose it? It gave great confidence to a soldier knowing his head, his brain, his thinking and his mind were protected.

Historical note — Roman combat helmets in the first century had large hinged side panels which adjusted to the soldier's face and also were tied with leather straps to keep it from coming off in battle. Our helmet of salvation is designed by God just for us and will perfectly protect us and will not come off no matter what the assault. When we understand that our salvation is of God and not human effort then we understand that a true believer is secure in the Lord.

Assurance of salvation protects our minds. We may face those who can kill the body but cannot touch our souls, that is in God's hands alone and He is not letting go. The knowledge of our salvation makes us free to fight without fear. It makes us more than conquerors.

Satan wants to plant the seeds of doubt in our minds and accuse us of not being true sons of God. He is a liar and deceiver. He wants to take away from us the peace and joy that comes from knowing we are God's possession. The knowledge of salvation gives us the assurance we need to face a difficult and cunning enemy.

> "These things I have written to you who believe in the name of the Son of God, so that you may know that you have eternal life." (1 John 5:13)

Putting on the helmet of salvation means to remind ourselves that when God saved us He did a forever work, something He will not undo.

> "Truly, truly, I say to you, he who hears My word, and believes Him who sent Me, has eternal life, and does not come into judgment, but has passed out of death into life. " (John 5:24)

## The sword of the Spirit. (Ephesians 6:17)

The first part of the Armor lists our protective gear. Now we come to a weapon. It is the most powerful weapon we can use in the spiritual war. God's inspired Word is that weapon.

> "For the word of God is living and active and sharper than any two-edged sword, and piercing as far as the division of soul and spirit, of both joints and marrow, and able to judge the thoughts and intentions of the heart." (Hebrews 4:12)

When Jesus was tempted by Satan in the wilderness He resisted and defeated the evil one by quoting Scripture. The Bible has power and authority that no word of man has. It will accomplish things we cannot.

> "... so is my word that goes out from my mouth: It will not return to me empty, but will accomplish what I desire and achieve the purpose for which I sent it." (Isaiah 55:10-11)

> "Let the one who has my word speak it faithfully ... "Is not my word like fire," declares the LORD, "and like a hammer that breaks a rock in pieces?" (Jeremiah 23:28-29)

It would have been a foolish and fatal mistake for a Roman soldier to go into battle and to have forgotten to take his sword or to leave it in its sheath and not use it. We should have the word of God with us at all times. One way is to have it in our memory. As we spend time studying God's word we are sharpening our sword for battle.

Just as a soldier trusted his sword so we must also have complete confidence that the Bible is the very inspired word of our Creator. It is fully trustable and we can use it with assurance that God is behind it and with it.

## All prayer. (Ephesians 6: 18-20)

The final theme of the book of Ephesians is prayer. It is both a weapon and an attitude. When we spend time in prayer we are saying to God, "I love You and just want to spend time with You."

In verse 18 Paul uses the word "all" four times.

> "**18 With all prayer and petition pray at all times in the Spirit, and with this in view, be on the alert with all perseverance and petition for all the saints,**"

For the body of Christ to be successful in the spiritual war of the two worlds, good and evil, there has to be a covering of prayer. This is not a part-time exercise, but it is a major commitment. It is about the church committed to all prayer, at all times and with all perseverance. It is for all of us, all the saints. Even though prayer is not usually referred to as a piece of the armor of God, it is definitely part of the overall battle plan and provides us with our marching orders from our Commander in Chief, the Lord Jesus Christ.

Paul then asks that the church pray for him that he will be bold for Jesus, never backing down in the conflict for the souls of men. We should be praying for one another in the same fervency and frequency that this passage challenges us

**Closing remarks. (Ephesians 6:21-24)**

> "²¹ But that you also may know about my circumstances, how I am doing, Tychicus, the beloved brother and faithful minister in the Lord, will make everything known to you. ²²I have sent him to you for this very purpose, so that you may know about us, and that he may comfort your hearts. ²³ Peace be to the brethren, and love with faith, from God the Father and the Lord Jesus Christ. ²⁴ Grace be with all those who love our Lord Jesus Christ with incorruptible love."

Paul was a prisoner in Rome and he did not want the Ephesian believers to be concerned for him so he sent Tychicus, a trusted co-worker, from Rome to Ephesus to encourage them. As encouraging as the letter to the Ephesians was, Paul wanted a personal word to accompany it from a trusted friend known to all the believers and one who had just been with Paul. It was very personal act. Even though he was unable to visit the Ephesians himself at that time, he was thinking about them and not his own circumstances.

Paul then ends his letter the way he began it, wishing them grace and peace and a desire that they know the great love of Christ in their lives.

**Amen and amen!**

# Summary and final thoughts.

The book of Ephesians is quite a journey. It begins with our incomparable God. Then man in his fallen, helpless condition is unveiled. "But God" enters the scene and rescues us. Mercy and grace overflow in Chapter Two. We, who were lost and hopeless, are lifted out of our pit of darkness and given light and life. We were adopted into the family of God. We then learn in Chapter Three how amazing that family is when a great mystery is revealed and explained. Jews and Gentiles have been forged into one church through the cross at Calvary. And so, Chapter Four begins with the unity God wants to see in the body and He helps us by giving us seven foundational beliefs where we need to be unified. Next, we discovered four special gifted people God has given to the church to help it grow in number and maturity. Apostles, prophets, evangelists and teachers were all given to the church for our benefit. The last part of Chapter Four and part of Chapter Five show us how a truly mature church acts. And then we are shown what mature relationships look like, from husband and wife, to godly children and finally to the workplace. Paul ends the epistle unveiling the unseen world of angels and demons and describes the spiritual war that is waging battle against our souls. He then concludes with the armor God has provided for our victory.

In the first chapter, I described the long passage about God and salvation like walking into a museum with many fascinating exhibits. As we conclude this brief overview of the book of Ephesians it has become clear that the entire book is a museum. It is the Museum of the Church. There are displays teaching us about God, sin, grace, salvation, the purpose of the church, our roles as members of God's eternal family and the war of the worlds that is ongoing. And it is a museum that is so vast and important that we will need to go back time and again to learn more and more.

And that is my final reminder. We will see new things in the exhibits each time we return to the Museum of the Church. There is just so much to see and our museum Guide, the Holy Spirit, is waiting at the entrance for you to show you around. Let's return often to the book of Ephesians.

# Notes

# Notes

# Notes

Made in the USA
Middletown, DE
10 May 2022

65440205R00097